The Shropshire Home Guard

This book is dedicated to my late sister,
Adrienne

The Shropshire Home Guard

by

Bernard Lowry

Logaston Press

LOGASTON PRESS
Little Logaston Woonton Almeley
Herefordshire HR3 6QH
logastonpress.co.uk

First published by Logaston Press 2010
Copyright © Bernard Lowry 2010

ISBN 978 1906663 46 9

Typeset by Logaston Press
and printed in Malta
by Gutenberg Press

Contents

Acknowledgements

A number of people have helped me and I wish to thank Armand DeFillipo and Kerry Dickin at Shropshire Archives, Peter Duckers at the Shropshire Regimental Museum, Bryan Heatley, Andy and Karen Johnson at Logaston Press, Colin Jones and Mick Wilks. In addition I wish to thank members and relatives of former members of the Shropshire Home Guard whose names can be found in the book. I also wish to thank my wife Geraldine for her patience.

Introduction

This book owes its existence to research I carried out for the national Defence of Britain project which began in 1995. It is not intended to be a detailed history of the Home Guard but rather a narrative based largely on documents held in the Shropshire Archives. Shropshire is fortunate in having an extensive Home Guard archive, something lacking in many other counties. This is not because the Home Guard existed without a bureaucracy, but rather, it seems, most paper records were destroyed at command and unit level after the Second World War. The bulk of the archived material relates to a number of battalions and their companies, meaning that some parts of the county receive little mention in this book. However, I hope that the book gives a 'feel' of what it was like to have been a member of Shropshire's Home Guard.

Although not situated in a part of the British Isles at risk of direct invasion from Europe, the Shropshire Home Guard had to be ready to fight an enemy which might seek to land from the sea on the Welsh coast and make for the Midlands, such an action probably being combined with airborne landings to capture vital airfields or to seize vulnerable points as part of a much larger operation.

The TV series 'Dad's Army' emphasised the less serious aspects of this citizens' army, but the image portrayed does less than justice to the memory of the Home Guard. Many of its members were already working long hours in their civilian role and yet were expected to turn out one evening per week and give up part or whole of their Sundays for parades, training courses or exercises. In addition, in the early days they were also expected to furnish patrols for the dusk to dawn parachutist watch. They were expected to take on new skills such as weapons training, map reading, field craft, battle craft and signalling. The officers, many of whom were retired veterans of the First World War, had to motivate their men and to deal with the considerable paperwork and general bureaucracy, and also to find the time themselves to go on lengthy and demanding courses.

The organisation reflected the class system of its time: the impression is that battalion and company commanders were invariably recruited from the ranks of those who lived in the local 'big house', but on the other hand these very men had had the necessary experience and responsibility of leading men in the previous war; as retired Army officers they were often impressively decorated for bravery. For example the commanders of the 1st Battalion (Lt Col Liddell), 2nd Battalion (Col Morris Eyton), 4th Battalion (Lt Col Dugdale), 7th Battalion (Lt Col Benson) and the commander of the Wellington Group (Lt Col Freeman) all held Military Crosses. It should be noted that the commanders of the battalions held the *official* rank of Lieutenant Colonel but in correspondence some, such as Colonel Morris Eyton, appear to have retained their earlier military ranks, albeit, perhaps, unofficially. I have used the titles by which officers are most frequently identified in the archival documents. The Home Guard was never straightforward!

There also appears to have been a little confusion in naming the Home Guard units, over whether to use the old county name of Salop or the more recent one of Shropshire. The organisation was usually referred to as the Shropshire Home Guard and its battalions were referred to either as the 7th Battalion Shropshire Home Guard or the 7th Shropshire Battalion Home Guard, but sometimes the old county name might be used as in the 7th Battalion (Salop) Home Guard. Sometimes the area where the battalion was based might be shown, for example the 5th (Wellington) Battalion (Shropshire) Home Guard. The county shoulder title showed an abbreviated form of Shropshire, simply the letters SHR.

There can also be confusion in the naming of the component parts of the LDV/Home Guard. Both were originally organized in companies, which in parts of the country could comprise 1,000 men. In August 1940, to make them less unwieldy, companies became battalions, the sections, into which the original companies had been divided, became companies, these in turn being subdivided into platoons. The companies would be led by a commander, a major or a captain, the platoons by a lieutenant.

Chapter 1

The Local Defence Volunteers in Shropshire

Britain has had a long and proud history of part-time soldiering stretching from the Anglo-Saxon *fyrd* to today's sophisticated Territorial Army. The modern volunteer movement, as opposed to earlier militias, began at the time of the Napoleonic wars when invasion seemed imminent. Volunteer infantry, cavalry and artillery units were formed to defend their own localities. These were disbanded at the end of the wars except for the cavalry volunteers, which became the Shropshire Yeomanry. Further fears of war with a France under Napoleon III and of invasion in 1859 led to the establishment of Volunteer Rifle Companies. In Shropshire, the 18 companies were later grouped to form the 1st and 2nd Volunteer Battalions of the King's Shropshire Light Infantry (KSLI), then becoming the 4th (Territorial) Battalion KSLI in 1908. The mounted element, the Yeomanry Cavalry, became the Shropshire Yeomanry Cavalry in 1872, converting to an artillery role in 1940. During the Second World War the Shropshire Yeomanry served in North Africa and Italy.[1]

In the First World War the idea of forming a voluntary corps of men who, for various reasons, were otherwise ineligible to enter the armed forces was mooted, leading to the establishment of the Volunteer Training Corps. No uniforms were initially available, only an armband with 'GR' on it, and the volunteers were assigned various duties which would free-up members of the Army, for example the guarding of vital installations such as ammunition factories and the providing of first aid parties. From 1916 onwards the Corps gained greater recognition and was assimilated into the military framework leading to the issue of a uniform, together with drill and weapon training,

The lapel badge of the First World War Volunteer Training Corps

the force eventually numbering a quarter of a million men. In Shropshire it consisted of two battalions, one based in Shrewsbury and the other in Wellington. At the end of the war the Corps was stood down.

In the 1930s, National Defence Companies, affiliated to local Territorial Army battalions, were organised using ex-servicemen who in time of an emergency would 'defend important points'. However, no training was provided nor adequate funds made available and the scheme was not judged a success, its members being absorbed into Home Service Battalions at the outbreak of war. Whether any such companies existed in Shropshire is not known.[2]

On 1 September 1939 Adolf Hitler invaded Poland: an ultimatum to Hitler to withdraw his troops expired at 1100 hrs on Sunday 3 September and on that day Britain and France found themselves at war with Germany. But before the actual declaration of war by the British Premier Neville Chamberlain, broadcast at 11.15am, a newly appointed special constable in Shropshire had had to warn German refugee farm labourers early on that morning not to travel more than three miles without police permission (all aliens, mainly people fleeing Nazi persecution, were required to be registered by the police under the Aliens Restriction Act of 1914).[3] For 13-year-old Glyn Rowlands, who would later in the war join the 1st Battalion Shropshire Home Guard at the earliest opportunity, the first intimation that war had begun was when, on that morning and as a choirboy in St Mary's Church in Shrewsbury, he heard the vicar, the Reverend Mackenzie, announce from the pulpit that Britain was at war. This left the congregation in a state of shock and no sermon was preached.[4]

Although France and Britain had gone to war to protect Poland, little in the way of offensive action could, realistically, be done in her aid and Poland soon collapsed. Germany sat behind her border defences with France (the incomplete West Wall or Siegfried Line), and France sat behind the powerful Maginot Line during a bitterly cold winter. Meanwhile, the British Expeditionary Force (BEF) which had been sent to sent to France was occupied building defences opposite the Belgian border. This 'phoney war' ended on 9 April 1940 with Germany's simultaneous invasion of Denmark and Norway. In the latter country the Germans demonstrated their use of air landed troops, capturing Oslo airfield and so enabling the bringing in of troops and supplies by air. The invasion the following month of Holland, Belgium and then France saw the Germans using transport aircraft together with gliders and parachutists to capture specific targets and outflanking their enemies. The rapid collapse of the French Army and the BEF was brought about partly by superior German equipment but mainly by superior tactics and strategies. The skilful tactics of leaders such as Guderian and Rommel, using armour to

A sight that was to haunt the British High Command and to tackle which the LDV was formed: German paratroops descend upon Holland on 10 May 1940

outdistance the enemy and dive bombers to silence opposition, defeated the once proud French Army and its British allies. If Britain was to be defended these tactics had to be mastered.

The shock of the new tactics was profound and one explanation given for the failure of the allies was the use by the enemy of a fifth column, a concern that also exercised the minds of Britain's defence planners in 1940. The phrase has its origins in the Spanish Civil War and represented the 'enemy within'. Although the Germans did resort to using soldiers dressed in Dutch uniforms to capture border posts, reports of parachutists dressed as nuns or in other disguises were totally untrue. However, a form of hysteria had set in: for example in May 1940 an unfortunate Belgian soldier, separated from his unit, was shot by French soldiers because it was felt that his unfamiliar uniform and guttural Brussels accent marked him out as a fifth columnist. Part of the role of the Local Defence Volunteers and the subsequent Home Guard was to be as an anti-parachutist, anti-spy and anti-fifth column force.

On 14 May 1940, the Secretary of State for War, Anthony Eden, on the day that the German Army crossed the River Meuse at Sedan, made a radio broadcast inviting men between the ages of 17 and 65 to enrol in a newly created force to be known as the Local Defence Volunteers. The intention was to raise a force of 150,000 men in

German paratroops, having landed, set up an MG34 machine gun

14 days to supplement the Regular Army's Home Defence forces, but so successful was the appeal that 400,000 enrolled.

In order to register for LDV duties a simple enrolment form was completed at a local police station which asked for details of the volunteer's nationality, occupation and any previous military service, and included questions such as 'Are you familiar with firearms?' and 'Are you prepared to serve away from home?'[5] Surprisingly, no questions were asked about any disabilities suffered by the applicant: as long as he possessed 'free movement' he was enrolled. It is said that one member of the Pontesbury LDV/Home Guard Platoon, who had been confined to a wheelchair for some years, was allocated the task of defending a bridge into the village, his only requirement being that he be pushed into position and be handed his shotgun![6] It is perhaps unsurprising that some at the time joked that the initials LDV stood for 'look, duck and vanish'. Three days later, on 17 May, the foundation of the LDV received Royal Assent under the Defence (Local Defence Volunteers) Regulations 1940.

The former headquarters of the Shropshire Zone Territorial Army Association on Claremont Hill, Shrewsbury

The volunteer, who was only required to provide part time service up until the time the force was mustered in the event of an invasion, and was not expected to live away from home, received no pay, although subsistence allowances were made where necessary. It was anticipated that the volunteer would serve for a term 'not exceeding the duration of the emergency', although he could volunteer for a set time. This changed when conscription was introduced in 1942.

Shropshire's commanding officers were chosen by the

county's Lord Lieutenant, the Earl of Powis, who worked in conjunction with the commander of the Army's North Wales Area, Brigadier Garnier. This area was divided into a number of Zones, Shropshire being number 6 and for which Lt Col G.P. Pollitt of Cressage, a farmer and a director of ICI, acted as Organiser of the LDV. Further appointments followed: for example, in the Wellington area on 18 May the Lord Lieutenant commissioned Lt Col H. Oldham to organise a battalion (initially called a group) which would operate over an area of 200 square miles, mainly agricultural in nature but also containing important industrial districts. The group was formed in two days, later being known as the 5th Battalion Shropshire Home Guard.[7]

Full use was to be made of Territorial Army Association resources: the county HQ in Claremont Buildings was responsible for administering and equipping the force, and existing drill halls, such as the Riding School at Coleham in Shrewsbury, were later taken over for use by the LDV's successor, the Home Guard. By 17 May 1940 the county already had seven LDV groups, each with its own organiser. Initially only those holding an appointment as a commander held a rank, this being indicated by bars on their uniform epaulettes. The Zone Commander had four bars, a Battalion Commander three, a Company Commander two and Platoon Commanders one. This form of insignia for senior officers was altered shortly after the formation of the Home Guard and, from 1941, army-style rank badges began to appear, together with proficiency badges and Home Guard years of service chevrons, whilst wound stripes could also be worn.

Representative of the early recruits into the LDV in Craven Arms were the two local bank managers, G.B. Shaw of the Midland Bank and M. Price of Barclays, together with F.B. Shaw who was a clerk in one of the banks. Of the 47 entries in a list of Craven Arms volunteers, whose ages ranged from 19 to 62, 24 had previous military experience including two who had been in the Officers' Training Corps. It was not unknown nationwide for highly decorated officers from the First World War to come forward and serve as humble privates.[8]

Brian Wright, who lived in Wistanstow, claimed to be one of the earliest recruits to the Craven Arms' LDV. Almost before Anthony Eden's broadcast had finished Brian walked to his local telephone box and called the police station in Craven Arms in order to give them his and his father's details as new volunteers. Major Holden of Sibdon was in charge of the Craven Arms LDV and appointed Brian's father to lead the Wistanstow LDV. His qualification for this appointment appears to have been that he was the local schoolmaster and had also served as a Bugle Major and as a Band Sergeant with the KSLI in India. Weapons initially consisted of shotguns owned by the recruits.

The Bridgnorth company included a man who had been born in October 1869 and who unsurprisingly was described as 'over age'. Another member was given permission not to march (or was told not to) as one of his legs was shorter than the other. One volunteer who had been born in August 1888 was described as a 'very awkward chap'.[9]

There was a real fear that the armed, albeit with shotguns, but un-uniformed LDV would be shot out of hand by the invader as *franc-tireurs* (terrorists) and so a 'uniform' of sorts was rushed out: an armband with 'LDV' printed on it. The first meeting of Wright's platoon was in the playground of the local school and a few days later they received their armbands. The 20 members possessed a few shotguns and cartridges, a couple of .22 rifles and Wright junior's air rifle. Their job was to watch for enemy parachutists from the high ground at Whittingslow, a bleak spot. So farmer Llewellyn Jones, the second in charge of the unit, put a chicken coop at their disposal as a form of shelter and this was towed up to the vantage point. Patrols of four men, rotating, carried out the watch from dawn to dusk. In Wright's group were Frank Davies, Joe Maund and Austin (Jack) Evans. It was a lonely business relieved only by the sight of the glow of railway fireboxes, despite attempts at masking, and lights displayed by the hooded headlights of vehicles as they went over bumps on the main road. Enemy air raids on the north-west of England were also visible.

Eventually, items of uniform started to trickle through but it was some months before all were fully uniformed.

Organising the men of the Craven Arms LDV was H.C. Meredith of H Division, No.5 Company, whose HQ was at Plowden Hall and who saw the role of his men as:

1. The protection of the area against paratroopers and other enemy troops intent on committing sabotage.
2. The rendering of all possible landing places unsafe.
3. If the enemy was too strong to tackle, then the military would be informed of their presence.
4. The blocking of all roads but avoiding hindrance to our own troops.

Any rifles and their ammunition (as they became available) were to be under the control of Meredith as commanding officer, and any men without were to have 'sporting guns with ball or buckshot'. The commander was also tasked with identifying 'danger points' and determining which vulnerable points needed protection.[10] To clarify what action needed to be taken imme-diately, a lecture was given on 2 June 1940 at Craven Arms where instructions were given on the obstruction of landing grounds by using the likes of farm implements and tree branches. It was emphasised that an enemy aircraft needed 600 yards in which to land, taking into account wind direction. A warning was also given that enemy paratroopers might make for railway installations and bridges, and may try to prepare advance landing grounds.[11]

To counter the threat from the sky, nightly patrols of three men plus a messenger were instituted in the Craven Arms area between 9.30pm and 5.30 am. The volunteers were to take their armbands, weapons and identity cards. No.2 Platoon, for example, patrolled the Colebach and Cefneinion area whilst No.3 Platoon patrolled the Bishops Castle and Aston area south of the bend of the Montgomery road. All over Britain similar patrols set out nightly with the intention of forestalling any threat posed by enemy parachutists and these would continue until such risks had been deemed to have passed.[12] However, this requirement did cause difficulties, especially amongst men already working long hours on farms, leading to one group of officers in the Craven Arms area writing and complaining that: 'We, the undersigned, who are keen platoon officers, find the operation of constant nightly patrols impossible at least until the enemy is expected. None of the men are not working all day, and therefore we cannot patrol all night [too].' The letter also mentioned that most of the men were middle aged. If a shift did not turn up, then the system broke down and there was, as yet, no compulsion on the men to turn out. The writers of the unsigned and undated letter made the suggestion that in future there should be one patrol operating one to two hours before dusk, with a similar patrol at dawn. They requested that the matter be discussed 'on Saturday morning'.[13]

In the event of mobilisation orders being received as a result of an invasion, members of the Craven Arms LDV were asked to proceed to the British Legion bringing with them their 'uniform' (which consisted of the field service cap, an LDV armlet and strong boots), plus a car or motorcycle if available. They were also to bring their weapons, ammunition, field glasses (if issued), spare petrol, a pick and shovel, a rope and an axe. The distributor arms of vehicles not brought to the mobilisation point were to be removed to prevent the vehicles' possible use by the enemy.[14]

In the north of the county, by 27 May 1940, LDV Group B No.1 Company, based at Ellesmere, had its HQ at the Police Station. The company consisted of two town platoons (I and II), together with two rural platoons (III and IV). The town platoons were to deal with 'action in any direction', whilst the rural platoons were to 'remain on guard in their own locality'. The objects of the LDV here were seen to be: the covering the country with a chain of observation posts, the guarding of vulnerable points 'depending on the number of rifles', and, if invasion came, the manning of strongpoints. It was recognised that this might prove 'unsound as there were no arms for additional men; and the life of the country would come to a stop', but the LDV would, *in extremis* and if not on duty elsewhere, 'man the barricades and with petrol bottles and brickbats do their best to inflict loss on the enemy'.[15] Although civilian cars were available in an emergency to form a mobile striking force, only six rifles and eleven sets of 'overalls' had been received to date and these had been issued to experienced riflemen only.[16]

In the same month a First World War veteran, Brigadier General Dann, who lived at Coton Hill, Shrewsbury and who was in charge of the town's LDV, wrote to the local paper stating that whilst a large number of men had already enrolled, all ex-servicemen should report to the Police Station as they would prove invaluable in training volunteers who had no past experience. A special appeal was made by him to motorcyclists and car drivers to make their vehicles available for LDV use, details of which could be handed in to the Police Station.[17]

By 19 May 5,000 men had enrolled in the county and within six weeks the country had one million volunteers.[18] But clearly, even ex-servicemen armed with the rare rifle or shot-

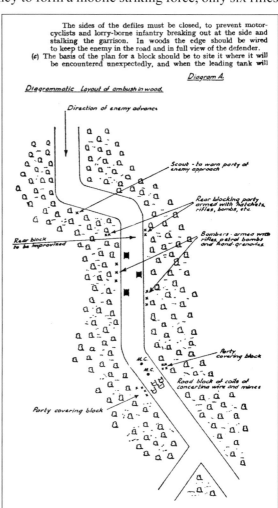

This page and opposite: Pages from LDV Instruction No.8 of 1940 'Tank Hunting'. Apart from small arms the anti-tank weapons to be employed (if available) were mines and 'petrol bombs'

gun could offer little resistance to the invader. Even so, by the end of May it was optimistically anticipated in the Ellesmere area that sufficient rifles would be forthcoming to arm all men proficient in their use, whilst men proficient in the use of the shotgun were to be armed with these, but if the rifles did not materialise then 'shotguns will be added'.[19]

This expectation was a little premature. Operation Dynamo, the evacuation of members of the BEF and French Army from Dunkirk, had begun on 26 May and went on till 4 June. But the army's artillery was left behind on the beaches. The initial need would be to rearm the Regular Army, and on 3 June agreement was reached in principle to acquire surplus weapons from the United States, together with machine guns and heavier equipment for the LDV. Once the necessary contracts had been signed, US freighters brought 500,000 .30 P17 rifles still in grease, together with 130 million .30 rounds of ammunition to the UK between the end of June and the beginning of August. The cost of buying these obsolete US rifles was, in 1940, almost $38m and had to be paid for by the UK out of its dollar reserves. It is little wonder, then, to learn that the UK's dollar reserves were exhausted by the purchase of arms and equipment from the USA by early 1941. To keep Britain and her allies fighting, the Lend-Lease Agreement of 1941 was passed by the US Government in order that more arms and supplies could be made available.[20]

In the late summer of 1940 the long-awaited US rifles began to appear. In August the commanding officer of H Company of

---

26	**NOT TO BE PUBLISHED**
G.S. Publications	The information given in this document is not to be communicated, either directly or indirectly, to the Press or to any person not holding an official position in His Majesty's Service.
338	

LOCAL DEFENCE VOLUNTEERS

INSTRUCTION No. 8—1940

TANKS AND TANK DESTRUCTION

1. The task

From the moment that enemy tanks are located they must be harried, hunted, sniped, and ambushed without respite until they are destroyed. Goliath was slain by David's sling, and the lessons of Spain and Finland confirm that tanks can be destroyed by men who have the bravery, resource, and determination to do so.

2. The German tank

The armoured fighting vehicle, for all its hard skin, apparent mobility, and armament, has serious weaknesses. Amongst these are:

(a) *Blindness.* The only view available is through the driver's slit, the gunners' slits, and the commander's slit, all of which are extremely cramped and the first at least fixed to the front. At any one moment, at least 90 per cent. of the surrounding country is invisible to a tank with a closed lid; it has no observation at all immediately above itself, and no observation whatsoever on the ground *within* a radius of approximately 15 feet of the tank itself. If a tank is not partially blind, but travelling with the lid open, rifle fire will soon make it close down.

(b) *Field of fire.* The guns are incapable of depression to fire on anything at ground level within an approximate radius of 20 feet of the vehicle or of elevations above 25 degrees. The tank cannot, therefore, engage targets in its immediate vicinity which are on the tops of high banks or in first floor windows of houses. The gun turrets revolve slowly, and their weapons defend the vehicle from attack only along their immediate line of sight. A simultaneous attack, therefore, from several directions finds serious gaps in its defence. A tank is incapable of firing into deep slit trenches at any range, except in enfilade.

(c) *Tracks.* The vehicle is mobile only as long as its tracks hold out. If it is forced on to rough or stony ground by blocks or demolitions, wear increases rapidly; and the tracks of the heaviest tanks have been broken by direct hits from our anti-tank rifle. Moreover, tracks can and have been removed from the heaviest type of tank by means of crowbars or wooden spars rammed in between the driving sprocket and the track whilst the vehicle was moving at a very slow pace. The British anti-tank mine will completely remove a track from any tank.

(d) *Crews.* The exhaustion of moving long distances and work for several hours in a closed tank is very considerable. The crews of tanks who have rested within an action require frequent rests for sleep and food, and are not super-men in any sense. For this purpose they halt in concealment harbours and lie about outside their vehicles.

---

what was later to be the 7th Battalion in south Shropshire instructed that all .303 rifles were to be delivered to his stables at Broadward House, Clungunford for packing and return to the War Office. The new rifles were issued with War Office instructions regarding their cleaning as they had arrived from the USA covered in preservative and their barrels full of grease. This course of action had been considered necessary, rather than cleaning at source, as the weapons were needed urgently. In addition to the rifles, other weapons purchased from the US for the LDV and Home Guard included Thompson submachine guns, Browning Automatic Rifles (often referred to as the BAR) and medium machine guns and Lewis machine guns (usually referred to as LMGs).[21]

With the arrival of US rifles and being the youngest in his platoon, Brian Wright was given the job of degreasing them. But despite the issue of the rifles, only five rounds per gun could be spared. And then one day a heavy box arrived: it contained a Lewis machine gun. This also had to be degreased, but there was only one magazine and little ammunition to fill it. Bottles were begged so that Molotov Cocktails could be made and Brian had the idea of putting the bottle inside a lady's woollen stocking and using this as a wick, an idea that was eventually passed on to the unofficial LDV/ Home Guard training school at Osterley Park in Surrey. At a time of austerity this idea might not have found favour with local housewives![22]

The massive loss of motor transport by the BEF in France also meant that there was no military transport available for the LDV in 1940 and so civilian vehicles would have to be used. From the Craven Arms LDV HQ at Plowden Hall in June, H.C. Meredith sent to a memo to Group Organisers (later to be known as Company Commanders) stating that: 'until battle positions are taken up unlicensed cars [those taken off the road by their owners for the duration of the war] will not be used for work in connection with the LDV but should be earmarked for whatever purposes are required and their owners provided with 'V's [a 'V' (for 'volunteer'?) sign placed on the left-hand side of the windscreen]. On the announcement of zero hour these vehicles may be used without a license and insurance.' A list of cars with their owners' details was to be kept by all Company Commanders, the greatest discretion was to be used in the issuing of 'V's and unlicensed cars were not to be used until the LDV was called out. Petrol coupons (rationing was in place) were to be supplied by the Territorial Army Authority.[23]

How the LDV, once armed, was to be employed was a matter of some continued confusion and much debate. On 5 June, General Ironside, Commander-in-Chief Home Forces, the man in overall charge of the defence of the UK, defined the role of the LDV in disarmingly simple terms as being: static defence, observation and reporting. Several confused training instructions followed, eventually leading, on the establishment of the Home Guard, to Training Instruction No.10 of 1 August 1940. By then General Alan Brooke had replaced Ironside and the force's functions had been redefined as:

1. Observation and the reporting of information.
2. Delaying and obstructing the enemy by any means in its power.
3. The protection of vulnerable points (VPs), such as factories, railways and Post Office systems.
4. Keeping a check on subversive activities.
5. Co-operation with the civil defence authorities.[24]

The fear of an air-landed enemy continued to exercise imaginations that summer. In south Shropshire instructions were issued to fire at 'the man not the parachute' if enemy parachutists were seen; it was believed that the idea of shooting at the parachute had been spread in the country by 'enemy agents'. A memo sent to the Shropshire LDV marked 'Secret' warned that parachutists might use gas, and also that they might appear to surrender 'but could have a grenade in each hand'. It was considered likely that they might try to land in any available space. A watch was to be made, too, 'for cryptic signs written on telegraph poles', and LDV volunteers were to watch for and to arrest anyone doing this and to hand them over to the police. It was also reported that 'several parachute harnesses had [already] been found in the Command area'.

It was also envisaged that German aircraft might try and damage the electricity grid by flying over power lines dangling wires which might cut or pull down power cables. Thus, any wires seen dangling from an overhead power line, which might have been severed from an aircraft, were to be reported.[25]

As the Battle of Britain gained momentum there was a realization that members of the RAF bailing out of aircraft might be assumed to be enemy parachutists, with unfortunate or even fatal consequences. In the summer of 1940 Shropshire Zone LDV wrote to Group Organisers setting out the procedure for dealing with RAF aircrew landing by parachute: these were to stand with their hands above their heads, fingers extended and to announce their identity loudly. They were to inform the LDV guard where their identity card was kept but not to lower their hands. If they were injured, they must lie flat.[26]

Meanwhile, in fields and open spaces all over the country obstacles were erected to stop enemy aircraft landing. Meadows alongside the Severn at Bridgnorth, for example, were obstructed by large concrete sewer pipes. At the same time there was an urgent need to maximise home food production during the Battle of the Atlantic and anti-Luftwaffe obstructions could harm this. Thus instructions went out that no obstructions were to be placed in hay or other growing crops without first contacting the farmer concerned. The need to maximise food production yet defend the country was to prove a source of continual irritation in agricultural areas such as Shropshire.[27]

On 22 June 1940 France signed an armistice with Germany. Britain, now alone, had to prepare for invasion. Along the coastline, around ports and harbours what guns were available after the withdrawal from Dunkirk were made ready. Airfields were prepared against air landings. A major 'stop line', the GHQ Line protected the south and east sides of the country with a network of subsidiary stop lines constructed elsewhere. These were built in the hope of delaying any advance from established beach-heads so that Army reserves could be marshalled and directed towards the enemy. In Shropshire, stop lines followed the rivers Severn and Teme and the Shropshire Union Canal. A number of pillboxes were built to protect important crossing points across the stop lines but these were not as thickly spread as in other, more vulnerable, parts of the country. In later defence plans large towns such as Shrewsbury were prepared for defence as anti-tank islands with the intention of denying the invader access to the important road and rail junctions which were then, in a pre by-pass and motorway era, located in such towns.

In anticipation of the invasion of Britain, Germany had drawn up, in August 1940, a military and geographic assessment of the country. For Shropshire the study noted the coalfields which existed in the area now covered by Telford, power generating plants at Ironbridge and also the importance of Crewe with its network of railway lines (the UK had a denser system than Germany), a number of which passed through Shropshire. The assessment deemed it unlikely that north Wales would be a suitable invasion area because of the scarcity of good harbours, the narrow coast roads, and the mountains which would have required the use of *gebirgsjaeger* (mountain warfare troops) – Western Command came to a similar conclusion but only in 1941. Modern industries were noted in the West Midlands, whilst Shropshire was generally noted for its farming (an army marches on its stomach!). The Severn was felt to pose a problem for crossing if flooded, and, on a further topographical note, 'particularly obvious natural obstructions are to be found in the mountains and ridges bordering the Midlands as well as the steeply rising north-eastern outliers of the Welsh mountains at Ironbridge'.[28]

To defend the Western Command area, III Corps was positioned to defend Wales, the West Midlands and the North West in July 1940. Woefully short of equipment, it contained two divisions – the 53rd (Welsh) and the 2nd

(London). Its HQ was at the Old Rectory in Whitchurch, the Commanding Officer being General Marshall-Cornwall who would, in 1941, take over charge of Western Command at its HQ in Chester Castle from General Finlayson. The Corps' responsibility was principally the defence of the area's beaches and open spaces against enemy air- or seaborne landings from the Mersey to the Bristol Channel, perhaps launched from Eire.[29]

In June and July 1940 there were continued alarms as invasion was imminently expected, although realistically Germany at this time was not in a position to mount such an operation after the losses she had suffered in the continental campaigns. On 2 July 1940 a memo was issued by Colonel Morris Eyton from Walcot Manor near Baschurch to officers of LDV Group B (later the 2nd Battalion) stating that 'the enemy attack would commence on 3 July with the LDV being relied on almost entirely for the static defence of the area'. Petrol pump handles were to be removed each night to deny the enemy fuel. This invasion, of course, never occurred.

On 5 July, Western Command, in Operational Instruction No.7, set out their defensive policy in detail. This was:

1. To prevent any hostile attempts at invasion by airborne or seaborne troops by the defence of all beaches with facilities for landing; by the defence of aerodromes and by the creation of obstacles on other areas suitable for landings.
2. To extend throughout the vulnerable parts of the Command a number of lines 'in which an enemy, advancing with or without tanks from east or west, will find no gaps or weak places and up against which he will be held firm until mobile troops can attack and destroy him'. Mutually supporting work would be carried out by the Royal Engineers, Home Defence Battalions and the LDV.

Attached to the Instruction was a list of 28 connecting stop lines, including No.1 which used the Severn from Tewkesbury to Llandrinio, No.8 which ran from the Severn outside Shrewsbury and along the Shropshire Union Canal to Nantwich (joining the Weaver), and No.28 which followed the Teme from its junction with the Severn to Ludlow.[30]

Yet there was continuing confusion as to the role of the volunteers. Colonel Morris Eyton of B Battalion issued a memo that the LDV were to be employed on:

1. Observation. (A subsequent Home Guard Instruction No.10 of 1940 noted that 'observation groups on church towers may carry observation and signalling equipment but not arms').

2. Manning obstacles.
3. The local defence of villages.
4. Guarding Vulnerable Points.
5. Anti-sabotage measures.
6. Assisting the police to control civilians.
7. Watching and harassing enemy troops.

The still scarce weapons, however, were to be handed from relief to relief at duty points.[31]

In July, S.R. Pollitt, Zone Commanding Officer, wrote and complained that some Battalion commanders were of the opinion that all efforts were to concentrate on rivers, canals and natural obstructions (presumably referring to stop lines). His instructions were that the LDV should only man the main defensive posts and roadblocks and should also defend their own villages. He expressed the interesting view that 'the enemy cannot manoeuvre mechanical transport in Shropshire except on the roads'. The LDV would therefore attempt to prevent the coming together of enemy groups and it was optimistically believed that every defended hamlet, even if only defended by one shotgun, could delay the enemy. On a more mundane level, he ordered that petrol bomb storage was to be 'small boy proof'.[32]

On 16 July, Colonel Morris Eyton wrote to his officers from Walford Estate Office informing them that 'The LDV is being relied on almost entirely for the static defence in this area. It is impossible to foresee if local field units will be moved off to fight elsewhere. The General Officer Commanding has absolute confidence in the LDV as long as they realise this and are properly armed. Support can only be relied upon from training units in the area. Refugees may be a great problem: the LDV are to work in close touch with the police and efforts were to be made to try to persuade civilians that they are much safer at home than on the roads'.

With this memo he also enclosed instructions on the signals to be used for stopping traffic. In daytime these were to be the normal police signal, but at night time a red lamp was to be swung or waved vigorously in addition to a vocal challenge. Twenty yards behind the man with the signal was to be another, ready to fire if necessary. These instructions appear to have been prompted by an order issued that month from the Army's North West Area HQ that complaints had been received concerning the lives of innocent motorists being put at risk due to their inability to understand instructions given by the LDV.[33] A list of garage owners in the battalion area was also issued at this time, and they were to be told to spoil their petrol in the event of an invasion, with pump handles being removed each night in the meantime.[34]

To help avoid an enemy masquerading as an officer of the LDV, another memo was sent from Walford Estate Office three days later requesting that all LDV officers down to Platoon Commanders were to be photographed at their own expense in uniform but without a cap. The photographs were to be sent to Walford as soon as possible and by 1 August the completed ID cards and photographs would be returned to officers.[35] On 11 August 1940, again fearing sabotage, Morris Eyton ordered that steel rail roadblocks were to be inspected regularly, kept clear of small stones and any tampering was to be reported.[36]

In addition to the fear of fifth columnists there was also a spy mania. Britain was in fact successful in entirely defeating the risk from enemy agents by a combination of luck, the vigilance of the civilian population and from the forced co-operation of some captured agents who were turned into double agents. A small number of agents did land on the UK's shores, delivered by parachute or seaplane. The first spies were two Norwegians who landed by parachute near Salisbury in September 1940, one, at least, of these being 'turned'. In April 1941 two further agents were 'turned', these having landed by seaplane off the coast of Scotland. Other agents who landed on our shores were not so lucky, 16 being executed during the war. It was not inappropriate, therefore, that one of the tasks of the LDV and Home Guard was the interception and apprehension of enemy agents, and vigilance had to be maintained.[37] Bill Wren from Oswestry joined the LDV on his 17th birthday on 5 June 1940 and recalls a jocular incident when his father received a report of a suspected enemy agent seen entering a barn at Vron Farm. The barn was surrounded by the armed LDV and the door kicked in. His father uttered the German equivalent of 'Come out, whoever you are' only to find that the intruder was an old tramp looking for shelter. So after that bit of excitement they decided it was time to go to the Barley Mow for a pint![38]

This multiplicity of roles was not solely the preoccupation of men. Some duties were handled by boys and women. Early volunteers in the Bridgnorth company included Joan Harborne, who worked as a civil servant (Ministry of Aircraft Production) at the Radio & Gramophone Development Company's factory, and Betty Reiman from Birmingham who was a radio tester at the same factory.[39] On 7 July 1940, B.R. Smith, a Section Leader, wrote from Trimpley, Ellesmere that Captain Cooper, a schoolmaster with Lancing College, evacuated from the south coast to Ellesmere College, was able to offer the services of two masters to perform dawn observation duties on 'The Tump' from 5am to 7am daily, together with three boys who would be watching from 9pm to 11pm. This would 'relieve the ladies of one hour in the morning and one in the evening'. It is clear that other women were also involved in such activities as on 26 September 1940, after the establishment of the Home Guard (see chapter 2), the local Home Guard commander wrote from the Drill Hall at Ellesmere a letter to a Mrs Dalby of the WVS expressing his thanks 'now that the ladies are to be released from their daily vigil on 'The Crimps'. He felt that the task could now be undertaken by the military and not by volunteers, but in his opinion the WVS had 'done [their] bit this summer'. Many women would later join the Home Guard as Auxiliaries, although the numbers were proportionately small in comparison with their male counterparts. For example, in July 1944 the 1st Battalion had just 18 women auxiliaries out of a battalion strength

The plastic badge issued to female auxiliaries in the Home Guard. This was the only item issued to the auxiliaries although in some parts of the country its members adopted their own, unofficial uniform

of 1,664. Little is known about their activities, but Major Jones in his history of D Company of the 2nd Battalion referred to a Mrs K. Ellis as Colonel Morris Eyton's 'right hand man'. There must have been many other women whose vital assistance to the organisation went unrecorded.[40]

Local clergy wanted to play their part too. The Territorial Army Association wrote to Colonel Morris Eyton of the 2nd Battalion on 23 November 1940 on the possible enrolment of the Reverend Pye of Colemere Vicarage into the Home Guard, possibly in a clerical or quartermaster capacity. Fans of 'Dad's Army' will remember the episode when the local Vicar ('his reverence') joined the Warmington on Sea Platoon, to Captain Mainwaring's annoyance.[41]

Episodes of 'Dad's Army' are also brought to mind in the reminiscences of Cyril Maddocks who was brought up on Coton Park Farm near Whixall and was enrolled into the 3rd Battalion of the Shropshire Home Guard (see below). Maddocks was called upon to use his family's car to drive officers to various meetings as cars were not that common in rural Shropshire. When it was realised that having too many officers in one car was not a good idea in case of an accident, they were spread between two cars. Members of his company included Tom Jones, a veteran of the First World War; and Frank Cartwright, a haulier whose cattle wagon along with the Bedford of another member, Bill Ford, was used to transport their company. Those wanting to go

Men of the No.4 Mobile Battle Platoon of G Company of the 3rd Battalion in June 1943. Cyril Maddocks is seated on the ground, second from the right. The seated man in the centre of the same row, in addition to having 'HOME GUARD' and 'SHR 3' badges on his left arm also has a badge lower down his arm which might indicate from its shape that he was a despatch rider. By this stage of the war the Home Guard was showing a distinctly soldierly appearance

into The Bull at Coton went in Frank's larger wagon, whilst those not wanting to stop off went in Bill's. Maddocks was too young to go into the pub, so Tom Jones, also a neighbour, would bring him a drink outside. Cyril remembers the difficulty of cycling to parades encumbered by his cumbersome bayonet on its leather belt, the awkward respirator case, the steel helmet and the bulky greatcoat. One item he had little time for was the Forage Cap which wouldn't stay on his head. Although the flaps could be folded down for warmth there still remained a big gap around the lower face. All in all he felt it was a quite impractical piece of headgear.

The LDV was soon to be renamed the Home Guard but looking back on the early days a member of the 11th Battalion (Wellington area) remembered that there was a rush of people to join the LDV, 'teachers and toilers, professionals and artisans'. He stated that some form of a skeleton organisation was improvised with little War Office material support, as weapons were practically unknown due to the catastrophic losses of the BEF at Dunkirk. But

Two Home Guard lapel badges,
that on the right being for the post-war Home Guard

he felt that this did not dampen the volunteers' ardour, all were keen to get going and shotguns were collected from their country owners. However, he recalled that the offer of an ancient muzzle-loading rifle was refused with thanks! Apart from a few revolvers, the only other weapons available were very elderly cavalry carbines covered in deep rust. Not surprisingly these were only suitable for training purposes. He went on to say that the quality of early training was very mixed, which was not pleasing to the old soldiers who were used to precise drill, but they gave their time to training those volunteers who lacked past military experience. 'Colonel Blimps' were unable to understand that the LDV/Home Guard were volunteers and he reported one officer as saying, during a lecture on the role of the LDV, that if any man failed to muster when Jerry landed, he would 'send two sergeants to fetch that man and have him shot'. His shocked audience were bemused when he then went on to ask for more volunteers![42]

Chapter 2

The Home Guard in Shropshire

In mid-July 1940, at Churchill's insistence, the force began to be referred to as the Home Guard (Churchill felt this to be a more patriotic and emotive title than Local Defence Volunteers) and on 23 July 1940 it became officially known as the Home Guard. To the commander of the 2nd Battalion, Colonel Morris Eyton, writing on 26 July 1940, the change of title would, in his opinion, make no difference as far as practical duties were concerned. In his view the name change was merely to provide a better newspaper heading. No general rank badges were to be issued, but officers' ranks would continue to be indicated by strips of braid on their shoulder straps.[1]

On 3 August all Home Guard units in Shropshire were affiliated to the county regiment, the King's Shropshire Light Infantry. At the same time the Groups became Battalions and the Organizers became Battalion Commanders, but there were still few rifles to equip the force.

At about this time an instruction was issued that the Home Guard was to cease the routine stopping of cars: it was felt that the exercise had served its purpose. In addition, if people were unable to produce their identity card when requested but had ample other proof of identity, they were to be allowed to pass. Military identity cards had already been issued to LDV officers in June. Security within the Home Guard was not always as tight as it might be as, in October 1940, the North West Area received reports that Home Guard orders were being placed in public places by certain commanders, and this had to cease immediately.[2] The concern about enemy agents had not gone away and the Army's North Wales Area issued instructions to the Home Guard that 'following the recent landing of agents in the country' more were to be expected and no opportunity must be given to them to dispose of any articles on their persons. A more immediate problem was, however, the number of foreign servicemen in the country with five different nationalities under uniform, requiring a memo to be issued to the Home Guard on ways of identifying foreign airmen.[3]

Whilst an adequate distribution of arms was awaited from the USA and in anticipation of the expected invasion, Colonel Morris Eyton, commander of B Battalion sent out a stirring notice on the 24 August 1940 that:

> Volunteers were urgently required to construct defences. Willing men and women should report with spades to the nearest Home Guard section or platoon. The matter is very urgent as recent intelligence received shows the enemy is making preparations for an airborne attack on this country within the next few days. Should an attack develop, civilians are to remain at home, and avoid using the roads. GOD SAVE THE KING.

He was clearly expressing the concern of the military of both being able to handle an airborne attack and the detrimental effect on troop movements caused by the massive flight of refugees on the roads of Belgium and France in the wake of the German attack.[4] That the threat posed by enemy parachutists continued to cause concern is shown in another operational order in August 1940, this time issued in the Oswestry Sub Area, that outlined the action to be taken against parachutists who, it was felt, were likely to be dropped in direct co-operation with attacks on aerodromes and landings on beaches. The Army Sub Area was to be divided into military districts in order to cordon off the parachutists. Church bells announcing the arrival of the parachutists were only to be rung in the affected area, where the senior Home Guard commander was to take control. He would inform the nearest military authority, call out the Home Guard to man posts on every road into the local settlement, where those attempting to enter would be examined, and was also to inform adjacent groups' platoons. He was then to take charge of a party to locate, pin down or capture the enemy and act as a guide to any mobile columns from the nearest military unit. At the same time he was to watch out for potential agents and saboteurs in civilian clothing whom, it was anticipated, would operate in small groups of four or five people.[5]

In October 1940, again in the Oswestry area, observation posts were mentioned as having been established by No.4 Company (West Felton) on Carreg y Beg and at Weston Rhyn. In addition, defence posts and road blocks were established on Oswestry Racecourse, The Llawnt, Cefn Coch, Hill Farm, Selattyn, Weston Lodge, Quinta Church, School Corner, the Holyhead Road and at the Chirk Viaduct. The latter was an important communications point and the subject of later Home Guard training exercises (see chapter 5).[6]

Men of the Hordley Home Guard, part of the 2nd Battalion (Salop) Home Guard, taken circa *late 1940. At least one man (excluding the vicar) has not yet received a set of the denim overalls his companions are wearing. Instead he has only received a brassard, cap and possibly boots. Other members have the leather gaiters in their as yet un-darkened finish. The man on the far left has had previous military experience as he has a ribbon bar. The wide variety of ages is also apparent.*
(Shropshire Archives)

A slightly later photograph of the Hordley Home Guard. By now most have been issued with greatcoats although these still bear the HOME GUARD brassard. Others have opted to wear the waterproof cape on this wet Sunday. (Shropshire Archives)

As time passed, the absence of any evidence for spies and saboteurs led to a slight relaxation in some duties, and Colonel Morris Eyton could write an instruction on 5 September that 'beginning from tonight, patrolling of the town will cease. Instead, three men per night would be on duty in the Drill Hall, and bedding would be provided.'[7]

The fear of fifth columnists had, however, not gone away. At the beginning of October the commander of the 3rd Battalion wrote from the Drill Hall at Wem on the subject of the 'Stopping of [an] Air Commodore'. This memo appears to have arisen from a complaint by a senior RAF officer about the manner in which his car had been detained. The battalion commander had been forced to make enquiries but he could find no member of his unit responsible for the incident, only that 'the air commodore was stopped by a special constable on the outskirts of Wem'. In any event, he went on, all the men of the 6th Company were out in uniform on the night in question and had definite instructions from their company commander to keep a good lookout for two parachutists mentioned in a message received from Market Drayton Home Guard, and any stopping of cars was done in the manner laid down in Home Guard instructions. Not only that, but owing to information received from the police regarding the parachutists, his men had been recalled and were back at their HQ before the incident happened.[8]

A further photograph of men of the Hordley Home Guard but including men from Lee and Tetchill, perhaps taken in 1942 or later. They now present a more uniform and soldierly appearance. Gaiters are now blackened and a number of the NCOs have medal ribbon bars indicating past military service

Episodes at roadblocks gave rise to many tales. Accounts of the Home Guard in Shropshire, in Charles Graves' *The Home Guard of Britain* published in 1943, relate how a patrol of the Wellington-based 5th Battalion found a drunken motorcyclist lying on the A5 and moved him into a ditch to sleep off his stupor. Shortly after this a colonel was stopped and asked to show his papers near the spot but he refused and became abusive when removed from his car. The patrol leader then ordered his men to 'take that … and show him what happened to the last chap who argued with us', referring to the motor-cyclist lying in the ditch! A First Sea Lord of the Admiralty, when similarly challenged on another occasion took a quite different approach and presented the patrol with 50 cigarettes for their keenness.

Another patrol came across a car in the early hours of the morning, and a reconnaissance of a nearby haystack provided sufficient information on the occupants' likely activities. The patrol duly withdrew but took a map, torch, and binoculars from the car, handing these to the police, the owner being thereby identified. Two weeks later the owner of the car, engaged in siting a roadblock, became overly forthright when discussing its layout. He quietened down when asked if he had found his map, binoculars and torch by the Home Guard Commander, a complete stranger to him!

Evidence for the continually changing role set for the Home Guard is seen with the Wellington-based 5th Battalion which saw its main operational role in 1940 as the taking of aggressive action against an enemy appearing in its area, plus controlling the important lines of communication. Suitable defence posts were reconnoitred, dug and developed with the help of the Regular Army.[9]

The 11th Battalion, in the Newport area, saw its whole force stood-to during the period when an invasion had seemed imminent, this activity perceived as having a beneficial effect on morale by achieving a greater sense of purpose. It was recorded that patrols continued after the climax was over, but this was a dreary period unless there were bombing raids in the vicinity, resulting in periods of 'utter boredom [interspersed with] brief phases of activity'. On one occasion flames were seen spurting up from fields as a result of incendiary bombs, the patrol stopping the flames from firing the nearby corn stacks after the stubble had ignited. At other times even the sudden appearance of a cat on a gatepost might be regarded as exciting! The picture changed with increased air raids. Later, when more training took place, it was said that map reading exercises were of universal interest as they often led to the nearest pub![10]

As has been mentioned, the ringing of church bells (which were silenced for all peaceful use during the early part of the war) was to act as a warning sign that parachutists had been spotted, but access to the bells could cause some problems in the summer and autumn of 1940. One church was known to have posted the sign: 'To ring church bells, key at vicarage'.[11] Other problems with the ringing of church bells arose after an incident on the night of 7 September. Called the 'Cromwell alert' after a Home Guard codeword that signalled that invasion by paratroops was imminent, this incident began as part of an anti-invasion exercise in another Command area that was inadvertently picked up by other Commands as the real thing. Brian Wright of Wistanstow recalls being wakened with the cry 'The Home Guard has been called out'. The invasion had started! He quickly donned his uniform and rushed to his invasion post, a 'knife rest', a moveable wood and barbed wire road barrier, by The Grove on the north side of Craven Arms and the road was blocked within minutes. His father put his unit on watches, with someone on the railway bridge over the Bishops Castle road where there was a cache of Molotov Cocktails ready to be dropped onto enemy tanks. The unit waited and, having had no further instructions, decided to go and report to The Grove where there was a KSLI training section, to be puzzled by the absence of any sentries – the KSLI soldiers had known nothing about the alert.[12] On the following day North West Area sent an instruction to the Shropshire Zone that Hofors (Home Forces) had reported that 'cases occurred last night where church bells were rung to call out the Home

Officers and men of the 11th Battalion at their Battle HQ at Harper Adams College. The three officers have the lapels of their battle dress blouses folded back to reveal khaki ties and one officer has a revolver with its lanyard around his neck. Again, some of the men have previous military service as evidenced by the medal ribbon bars

Guard. Orders are that bells are <u>only</u> to be rung if parachutists are seen in the area – the signal is <u>not</u> to be taken up in adjacent areas.'[13]

Worries about parachutists could also cause false alarms. In another tale from Charles Graves' *The Home Guard of Britain*, a Shropshire Home Guard commander was called to an RAF station at 4am by his Commanding Officer to discuss a report of descending parachutists. On visiting his observation post it was found that the parachutists were merely barrage balloons being hauled down, glinting in the early morning sun!

Whilst the Home Guard watched and waited in the late summer of 1940, Hitler continued to mull over Operation Sealion, the invasion of Britain. In the event Hitler was not that enthusiastic regarding the operation despite the Wehrmacht considering that it would merely be an 'extended river crossing'. The Luftwaffe would have to have total air control over the landing areas in order to protect the vulnerable invasion craft (both ships and aeroplanes) from the RAF. It would also have to help prevent the Royal Navy from destroying the seaborne armada. The invasion fleet would have to move at night on a flat sea and land at dawn. Germany was aware of Britain's anti-invasion measures from aerial reconnaissance. In the event, the Luftwaffe failed to gain mastery of the air during the Battle of Britain and, given the relative lack of enthusiasm for the operation, Sealion was quietly postponed on 17 September 1940, although this was not known to Britain. In any event, soon after the defeat of France, Hitler was turning his thoughts to his ideological enemy, the USSR. In the meantime, Hitler believed Britain could be isolated, bullied or starved to the negotiating table by the U-boat war. Once the USSR was defeated (its rapid collapse was predicted by Hitler) there would be plenty of time to turn Germany's attention back to Britain.

Unaware, of course, that the invasion had been postponed, Morris Eyton's battalion received a Western Command instruction on 23 September 1940 regarding 'tank hunting':

> To cope with the possible invasion, one or more Tank Hunting Sections are to be formed by each Home Guard Battalion. Each Section is to consist of one Section Leader and nine men and as many spare men as can be trained. The Section's armoury will consist of Molotov Cocktails, one Lewis gun, rifles, one axe for tree felling and two light crowbars (to be acquired locally). No transport is deemed necessary, personnel can make use of cycles. No further equipment would be available and carriers for the Molotovs are to be improvised locally. Each Section would operate within a five mile radius. Their role is to stalk, surprise and destroy hostile tanks and their crews so preventing them reaching the larger towns and cities. All Battalions have sections

formed to deal with parachutists and the tank hunters are to be trained on similar lines.

Even so, fear of invasion gradually receded as the winter of 1940 approached, and Brian Wright noted that by late 1940 the nightly watch had been abandoned for the time being. Comfortable quarters had been found by Wright and his colleagues in an outhouse at Bushmoor where beds and cooking facilities were rigged-up. Their role now was patrolling and looking for possible saboteurs along the railway line. He could remember little rifle-firing training during his time in the Home Guard, but in April 1941 he passed into an Army Young Soldiers Battalion. His experiences had proved useful in that, at least, he already possessed a uniform 'with creases in the trousers, a shape in the cap and boots that had softened somewhat'.[14]

As time passed there was more regularisation of the organisation of the Home Guard: in September 1940 an instruction from the General Staff Home Guard North West Area to Walford Manor noted that the platoon establishment was to consist of one platoon commander with one sergeant or other NCO. Each platoon was to have four sections of ten men, one of which was to be a Lewis Gun section. The 'number one' of the Lewis Gun would be the Section Leader. Four other men were to carry rifles or shotguns and the gun equipment. One man was to have a cycle. The three other sections were to

The former Shropshire Yeomanry Riding School in Shrewsbury, now demolished. In mid war this replaced Morris House on Wyle Cop as the 1st Battalion's HQ

consist of men each with rifles or shotguns. Each platoon was thus to have approximately 48 members, but many men were still not yet armed.[15]

Gradually the aim of the force came to be to defend specified localities, as is indicated in an instruction from Walford Manor to all the battalion's companies dated 7 October 1940:

> Each company commander will divide his area into two, three or more fortified camps corresponding to the platoon administrative area which was originally formed on quite different principles. The boundaries of each of the fortified camps will be governed by tactical features e.g. roads, canals and conformation of the ground.
>
> Every road entering such fortified camps will be barred by a light series of field fortifications and some device such as a cable capable of being put rapidly into position. Where natural tank obstacles e.g. rivers or canals exist defences will be made at these points, otherwise they are to be put where the greatest economy of manpower can be effected. Within the perimeter of each camp, each defence post will be the responsibility of the nearest section leader who should take the greatest pride in making his own particular position really effective. Defenders will come from within the inside of the camp.
>
> Digging in, wherever possible, rather than using sandbagged walls, is the method to be adopted and some of the fire positions must be well out to the flanks. By this means contact may often be maintained with the next defence post, perhaps half a mile away.
>
> The platoon leader will be responsible for co-ordinating the several defence posts in his camp and in battle for keeping the company commander informed of the position.
>
> Each section leader will assume complete responsibility for his own sector of the defences and should the enemy show signs of an outflanking manoeuvre, he should be prepared to move some men rapidly to the threatened flanks where contact with the next post will be obtained. Before any really effective field operations can be carried out these defences must be completed.[16]

The above instruction notes the use of cables, in effect often those redundant from colliery winding gear. These were to be used to quickly block-off roads to light enemy reconnaissance vehicles such as motorcycle combinations and scout cars. There are details of their intended use in Ellesmere in October 1940 where twelve cables were required for the Swan Hill-Cremorne area (requiring a total cable length of 210 feet): four for Lion Lane (47 feet), two in Crossfields (42 feet), four for the Lyneal Canal Bridge (75 feet), four for Black Coppice (80 feet), four for Winston Farm (55 feet), four for Tetchill

Moor Lane (66 feet), and two at Lee Reeves Farm (39 feet). A total of 36 cables were therefore ordered for the defence of the town.[17]

The advent of 1941 brought an increased emphasis on training. The question of training is covered more fully in chapter 5 but the following is an indication of the increased effort being put into the subject at this time. The commander of the 7th Battalion wrote, on 13 January 1941, that the Army Junior Leaders School at Ludlow were proposing short Sunday courses in musketry; the duties of the sentry; concealment and cover; field craft; anti-gas; the Mills Bomb; fire control; map reading, and the laying of landmines. Although the Home Guard at this juncture had no anti-tank artillery, anti-tank mines nevertheless constituted a simple and potent anti-tank weapon in all armies up to the end of the war, and beyond. Haversack rations were to be brought to the courses, and a subsistence allowance would be paid for those away from home for over 12 hours.[18]

There was some concern as to who should provide the training, and the commanding officer of C Company of the south Shropshire 7th Battalion received notice that 'certain persons without military status were offering their services to the Home Guard but these were not to be accepted without proper enquiry'. Lecturers approved of were Sir Michael Bourne, who offered to lecture on the Browning machine gun and automatic rifle, Roland Penrose on camouflage, and John Langdon Davies, who wrote on defence matters for the *Sunday Pictorial*. The last two had lectured at an unofficial training course at Osterley Park in Surrey, organised by the owner of the periodical *Picture Post*. Osterley Park was eventually closed by the War Office as the military and political establishment were wary of some of the lecturers, especially the communist Tom Wintringham (see chapter 5).[19]

In addition to lectures, field exercises were organised. An early one appears to have been a tactical exercise held on Sunday 19 January 1941 where the scenario (known to the Home Guard as a 'scheme') was that parachutists had been seen descending in the Clun and Bishops Castle area. The Home Guard was to pin them down and 'do them in if possible to prevent them reaching their objectives'. The 'enemy' was to be represented by Army personnel from Walcot with the flaps of their forage caps buttoned under their chins. Rattles would represent machine guns. The Home Guard was to show their presence by holding the butt of their rifles above their heads. On locating the 'enemy' and if unable to 'do them in', a message was to be sent to Lydbury House (Company HQ) for the Army machine gun squad to be sent from Walcot.[20] In a review of the exercise dated 16 February there was some criticism. For example, 'disguised civilians were not carefully searched and these could do a lot of damage' (presumably as fifth columnists). A private car was left and not immobilised, which could have been used by the 'enemy', especially as it was also found to contain a revolver and a plan of the attack. The criticism regarding the searching of civilians was not wholly accepted by the Home Guard recipient as a comment was added wondering how far they could go in checking whether ladies were genuine.[21] There is more detail on this exercise in chapter 5.

As for the organisation of the Home Guard, in early 1941 it was agreed to grant commissions to officers and over 500 were given in the county by a selection board presided over by Sir Charles Grant, the Colonel of the KSLI. In the same year Lord Bridgeman, a Shropshire man, became Director General of the Home Guard. In March 1941 the introduction of Warrant and NCO ranks occurred. Whilst none of these developments carried any financial benefit, the Home Guard was gradually becoming more on a par with the Regular Army.

As 1941 advanced, thoughts again turned to the probability of invasion. In February, an Oswestry Sub Area Operational Order gave a list of posts to

Officers and men of the Sentinel Waggon Works Home Guard, Shrewsbury. The men would have provided patrols against possible sabotage attack. The special ammunition pouches provided for the Home Guard can be seen on the figures at the extreme margins of the group. The front of the building has been covered by a large camouflage net. In the Second World War the company produced items such as bren gun carriers and ammunition cases. The carriers were tested on Haughmond Hill and those designed for wading were tested in a pool within Ebury hillfort. The concrete roads, hardstandings and ramp into the pool remain visible

be manned by the 7th Heavy Anti Aircraft Regiment based in the area in the event of invasion. A plan was drawn up whereby, if the evacuation of civilians became necessary, 'Red' and 'Blue' roads were to be kept clear for the use of military transport. The regional Traffic Control Office was at Foregate House in Shrewsbury.[22] Yet materials and the wherewithal to construct and man defences was still lacking. One officer in the 7th Battalion area (south Shropshire) wrote upon a memo he had received advising on and urging the sandbagging and barbed-wiring of defensive positions: 'Fatuous. When will the materials be available?'[23]

Early 1941 also saw Colonel Morris Eyton at Walcot setting out his thoughts in a manner that was critical of his superiors:

To all ranks 2nd Battalion Shropshire Home Guard.
The flood of oral and written advice to the Home Guard has made it desirable to set out the objectives of the 2nd Battalion. Not one of the advisers has taken the trouble to enquire as to our objectives, fire power, nor the extent of the country our fire power has to cover. Only one officially recognised VP [vulnerable point] is in our battalion area.
It seems certain, apart from bombing, that enemy action will take the form of raiding parties landed as a diversion to attack elsewhere, charged with the destruction of objectives outside our area.
It is anticipated that the Luftwaffe will land parties of 200 men to cause the maximum dislocation, fending for themselves. Such a landing would test severely the Home Guard. Whether tanks would be landed is obscure – the battalion commander feels these would be few in number and very light. It is more likely that the landed parties would try to seize transport to make for their objectives, and rely on surprise rather than on tanks which carry few passengers. The objective of the Battalion is clear: the prevention of the passage of enemy troops across the Battalion area.
The only possible plan is to have as many pickets as possible astride every road at intervals of a few miles so that contact with the enemy is certain. Reinforcements are to form a continuous front. Since the Maginot Line, the view is that anything in the nature of a line is doomed to failure, regardless of conditions. In the Battalion Commander's view, this has been overdone. The Maginot Line was not penetrated but outflanked. [My] view is that the BEF line held and the misfortunes were largely due to our allies. In any event no alternative can be proposed for our troops with the limitations of the Home Guard in the matter of offensive weapons, training and transport.
Each Company therefore will, unless and until ordered by a higher authority, see that their men are disposed of above according to the plan above. The only exception is in respect of an affected Platoon

where the Leader will collect every available man and attack; prompt action may prevent casualties as the enemy may be unprepared.

It is not expected that the telephone services will function normally when the invasion is underway. Companies are to rely on quick wits etc. The Battalion Commander will do what he can, but delegation will be necessary.

There is the question of the enemy's new weapons: gas, death rays and many marvellous inventions. The Battalion CO will always keep both feet on the ground, and has made some bitter enemies as a consequence, especially among those whose minds work differently.

Despite a general move away from stop lines towards defended localities, anti-tank islands, nodal points and centres of resistance, at least one Home Guard commander was still attached to the idea of linear defences.[24]

As defence moved towards defended localities, Ludlow, Bridgnorth, Donnington, Wellington, Newport, Shrewsbury, Pontesbury, Much Wenlock, Whitchurch, Whittington and Oswestry were declared anti-tank islands, to be defended from tank attack from all directions. Other towns were named as nodal points and also given defences, including Church Stretton, Craven Arms, Ellesmere, Wem and Market Drayton. There was a certain amount of fluidity in definition and purpose, and some localities, such as Whittington, lost their status as anti-tank islands. The smallest centres of population often became 'centres of resistance'. In every case a detailed study took place and plans were drawn to show the defences based on Army guidance.

The renewed fear of invasion in the spring of 1941 led to more spy mania. In the Oswestry area an exercise took place over the nights of 24 and 25 February in which a list of the names and addresses of all those out travelling was to be taken. No one was to be detained unless there were strong suspicions by the Home Guard NCO, but any suspect was to be handed over to the police who, it was hoped, would also be at each roadblock. Rifles were not to be loaded and traffic signal lamps were to be taken. Fire engines, police cars, and civil defence vehicles were to be allowed to pass through with the minimum of inconvenience. Roadblocks were established at Welshampton (Station Bridge) and at Overton Road (Grange Road post). It was reported after the exercise that civilians without their gas masks numbered 394, whilst those without identity cards numbered 249. It was felt that the roadblocks were well sited and lighted and there was no danger to traffic.

However the general population were becoming increasingly frustrated at having their identities continually checked and by the middle of 1941 only 'unknown' persons were to be checked.

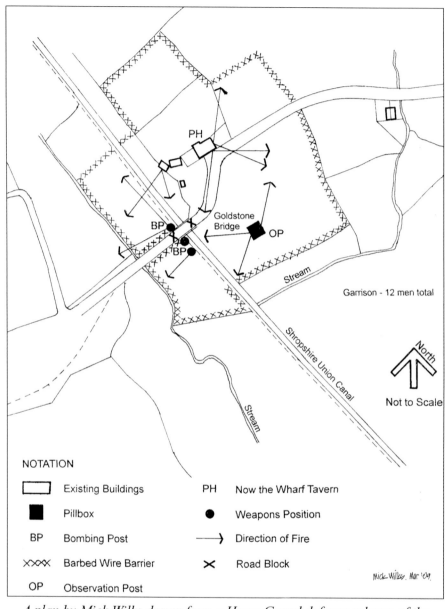

NOTATION

▭	Existing Buildings	PH	Now the Wharf Tavern
■	Pillbox	●	Weapons Position
BP	Bombing Post	⟶	Direction of Fire
✕✕✕✕	Barbed Wire Barrier	✕	Road Block
OP	Observation Post		

*A plan by Mick Wilks drawn from a Home Guard defence scheme of the
defended locality at Goldstone Wharf on the Shropshire Union Canal (SUC)
near Cheswardine. In 1940 a pillbox was built to command the crossing as
part of the SUC invasion stop line. The defence scheme incorporates the
pillbox into the later war philosophy of anti tank-islands, defended localities
and centres of resistance*

There was still concern about spies, nonetheless, and a memo on the subject was sent from Walford Manor to all battalion companies on 21 March 1941. Spies were expected to appear at any time and more likely to arrive by parachute than by boat, and were thus likely to be young. It was suggested, therefore, that anyone suffering from minor injuries which could have resulted from a parachute landing might be worth a second look. Likewise anyone with a foreign accent, although it was acknowledged that there were a large number of refugees in England. If the individual didn't know where he was, or had foreign-looking clothing this was to be checked. Might they have a wireless set disguised as a suitcase? Certainly anyone in possession of a quantity of money, foreign chocolate or cigarettes, a map or compass, or two ID cards was to be treated as a suspicious character.[25]

In respect of enemy parachutists, the question of the ringing of church bells returned again in March 1941. An instruction was issued that it was everyone's duty to ring the bells if six or more parachutists were seen in the area, although it ought to be those Home Guard members manning observation post that should spot them first, and then ring the bells. The authorities had arranged procedures with the bishops so that their clergy should co-

The Home Guard defended locality at Goldstone Wharf with the canal bridge in the background. In the foreground still remain some of the concrete cylinders which would have been placed on either side of the steel rail barriers on the bridge. They now provide a convenient means of stopping cars driving off the Wharf Tavern car park and into the canal

operate with the Home Guard and it was felt that there was no need for the clergy to have to refer to a commanding officer for authority for the bells to be rung. But there did need to be someone available who knew how to ring the bells![26]

Gradually the various Home Guard platoons were focusing on defending selected points, be these communication junctions (nodal points), vulnerable points such as the approaches to airfields, factories and power stations, places where an advance could be held up at a stop line, or settlements that had been turned into anti-tank islands. By April 1941 the Wellington Home Guard had established defences and trench systems at Barnfield Farm buildings ('No.3 and first LG [Lewis gun] team'), Wrekin post road block, Oasis, Wasps Nest, Pavilion, Hayfield, Bullring, Lane End, School Corner, Salop Bridge/ Drayton Bridge (railway platoon), Ross Point-Cottage Pie-Arrowhead (No.2 Section)

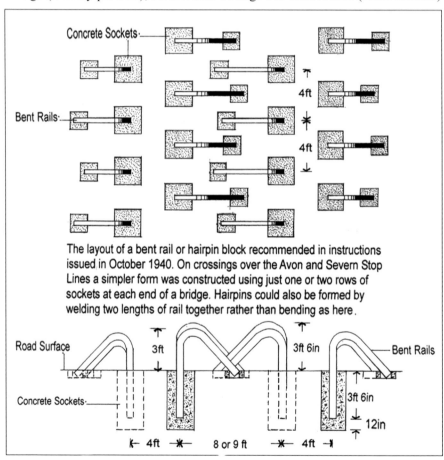

The layout of a bent rail or hairpin block recommended in instructions issued in October 1940. On crossings over the Avon and Severn Stop Lines a simpler form was constructed using just one or two rows of sockets at each end of a bridge. Hairpins could also be formed by welding two lengths of rail together rather than bending as here.

Section through a bent rail or hairpin roadblock

and at Dothill. It is possible that some of the above may represent codewords for some positions.[27]

Following the crude roadblocks of 1940, substantial anti-vehicle and anti-tank blocks were introduced. Often a steel cable was erected across a road, of sufficient size to halt German motorcycle reconnaissance troops, light vehicles and armoured cars. Then came the anti-tank obstacle proper, normally erected on a bridge or in some other confined area. This would block an approach from either direction and be covered by fire from Home Guard troops to prevent its removal whilst also attacking the enemy. The components were a number of concrete cylinders at either end between which were steel uprights or hairpins and large girders set into prepared, covered sockets in the road surface. The roadblocks were to be erected only once the enemy were in the area, with the Home Guard remaining under cover. 'Bombing pits' were to be manned by one or two men with other men behind hedges with rifles or submachine guns, with a reserve to cover the flanks. Attempts at manning such defence posts could be vitiated by familiarity. Following an exercise in March 1941 in south Shropshire where hairpin roadblocks were to be erected, the Home Guard were instructed that they must make sure that socket covers were removable as these had had to be removed 'after hours of work with pickaxes and metal bars'. When such posts were erected and manned, the guiding principle as regards checking civilians or mili-

Surviving staggered sockets with covers for anti-tank rails by the castle in Ellesmere

tary personnel who wished to pass through was that 'no undue delay is to be induced, so there is to be no examinations where individuals are known'.[28]

In May 1941 observation posts were recorded in the Oswestry Battalion area at Ellesmere (Welsh Frankton Church); Baschurch (on Harmer Hill and The Cliffe); Knockin (Nesscliffe); Queens Head (Queens Head Hotel); Gobowen (Ifton Colliery Fosse); Oswestry (Racecourse) and at Llanforda (Sweeney Mountain and Moelydd). These were reported to be manned from 9pm to 7am. Whilst the Home Guard made use of churches such as that at Welsh Frankton for observation, this was on the understanding that no firearms were to be taken into the buildings.[29]

Home Guard anti-tank block at The Cartway, Bridgnorth. In the foreground are the sockets (with covers) for the bent steel rails (hairpins) seen to the left of the cyclists. Beyond the rails is a long row of concrete cylinders which would have been placed on either side of the double row of rails. Some pieces of rock lie against the bank: these would have been spread amongst the cylinders to prevent them being overturned and acting as a roller when struck by a tank. It is likely that a bombing post would have been situated on the top of the sandstone bank

Bill Wren from Oswestry joined the Home Guard on his 17th birthday on 5 June 1940, and his father, who had had previous military experience, was appointed commander of the Trefonen Platoon. In the early days, he recalls that farmers brought along shotguns and drilling took place in School Lane with broomsticks for rifles. Later, US .30 rifles arrived. A strongpoint was set up on The Cross at Trefonen. Steel hawsers were anchored to a large tree in the grounds of the local inn which were then looped around a stone post on the opposite side of the road. A slit trench was dug by the War Memorial and there were probably other obstacles such as cylinders and steel rails. The Old Band House became the local Home Guard HQ with an observation post on Mynydd Myfyr to the north-west of the village.[30]

Construction of observation posts and defences often caused friction with farmers and on 14 May the following Army instruction was issued:

> Entry and work on private property: HQ Western Command report numerous complaints from farmers when members of the Home Guard enter land without permission and therefore without the issue of a Notice, and proceed to dig defence works, erect wire entanglements etc. This is of inconvenience to the farmer and detrimental to food production. Without the issue of the Defence Regulations Notice the farmer cannot seek redress for any loss or damage.
>
> When time permits, proper Notice is to be given, with pro-forma, to the War Office Land Agent.
>
> In every case written Notice of intention is to be given and this must state the name and address of the Agent: Capt L.J.R. Taylor, School Chambers, School Gardens, Shrewsbury.
>
> There is a general need for consultation – in some cases involvement of the Ministry of Food is to be considered.

This was followed the same month by a further memo entitled 'Defence works on private property'. This allowed a Home Guard officer, of the rank of Major or above, to sign a pro-forma notice in the absence of a Royal Engineers officer, the notice reading as follows: 'Take notice under Regulation 50 Defence of the Realm Act 1939 it is necessary to do the work specified below on land owned or occupied by you at [location]. A compensation form may be sent if desired. Send this to the Command Land Agent, Western Command, Chester. [Signed] C.E.P. Sankey Lt Col RE [Royal Engineers] CRE [Commander Royal Engineers] North Wales Area.'[31]

The flow of memos and instructions also show that there was a gradual change in the official attitude as to the effectiveness of pillboxes. Although many thousands had been built in the summer of 1940, mainly to provide defences along the stop lines, a Home Guard Instruction dated 27 June 1941 noted that pillboxes were difficult to conceal, an obvious target for enemy guns, and had restricted vision from within enabling the enemy to 'stalk' and to get close unseen. For this reason they were to be considered as temporary shelters in time of trouble, and most of the local garrison should be outside in entrenched positions or in houses reinforced with sandbags and barbed wire. Those pillboxes considered to be badly sited were to be used as dummies to attract enemy fire.[32]

In the same month the earlier predictions of small groups of four or five enemy parachutists landing was being reconsidered. This is likely to have been influenced by the invasion of Crete by large groups of German air-landed forces. The small, numerous defensive positions previously constructed were now no longer likely to be of much use. A memo ordered that stronger defence posts on important roads and other strategic positions should now be constructed. The concept of the linear defences of 1940 was now dying as the 'impossibility of forming continuous lines across the country was now being recognised'. Added to this memo by one of its recipients, a 2nd Battalion company commander, was the terse comment: 'What about stop lines – washed out?'[33]

A Western Command Instruction of August 1941 on the obstructing and delaying of the enemy further mentions this new defence concept, whilst not yet wholly moving away from the concept of linear defences:

> There are not enough Regulars to man all of the stop lines but these are of the utmost importance in order to prevent different enemy landings from joining up and so forming a large concentration, and making such difficult to break up and defeat. The Home Guard are to help man stop lines but some members … say that this is not their job and want the bulk of the Field Army as mobile reserves to dash at the enemy. Therefore it is left to the Home Guard to man, to the utmost possible extent, defended localities and vulnerable points. It is a mistake to underestimate the value of continuous anti-tank obstacles, for example rivers, when used in conjunction with a network of defended localities.[34]

On Marshall-Cornwall's move from Commander of the III Corps to that of the Western Command area based in Chester in late 1941 there began a change of emphasis: the risk of sea landings in the area was now felt to be unlikely, and emphasis switched increasingly to defence, in the first instance by the Home Guard, against airborne landings on vulnerable points such as airfields, together with an emphasis on a high level of mobility for the few and scattered Home Defence troops scattered around the Command area. This review might also have been undertaken in view of Red Army reverses in the Soviet Union. The impact on the civilian population was also considered.

In the Oswestry Sub Area Defence Scheme No.2 can be seen the movement towards stronger but fewer defended localities. The scheme anticipated the landing of parachutists in isolated detachments, combined with enemy seaborne detachments and countrywide operations on a larger scale. The Home Guard role was now seen as: observation, the pinning down of the enemy and the static defence of nodal points. The object was 'To canalise enemy movement by holding selected defensible towns and large villages that the enemy cannot capture without a full scale attack. The Home Guard are to resist whilst they await the arrival of troops'. It was not seen as practicable to hold small posts, rather that if the Home Guard withdrew from these it 'will save the life of the villagers'. Company and platoon defended localities were to hold even if the enemy got past. Concealment was to be the watchword. Somewhat later, on 7 November, a further instruction from the Oswestry Sub Area emphasised that: 'The defence of the inner perimeter or keep of nodal points is to be to the last man and round and the blocks will, if proper hairpin blocks are not provided, be made as strong as possible with vehicles, boulders etc.'[35] The 'keep' usually consisted of a substantial building or, in a large town, a collection of buildings near to the main transport junction that was to be held to the last man and round,

Not all defences were very sophisticated. An undated defence plan ('Number Two') marked 'SECRET' set out the defence of Pontesbury in the area of the 4th Battalion. The company HQ was in the Railway Inn. One NCO and six men were to be on the railway bridge outpost over the Minsterley road, their duty being to block the road with 'trucks filled with stones' when the necessary orders were received. The trucks would then be run down the line and toppled onto the road. 'Tanks would be attacked with grenades and after doing as much damage as possible the outpost is to retire on the remainder of the platoon who would be covering them ... If the attack is successful F3 Platoon would be ordered to support F1 Platoon to harry and delay the enemy. After inflicting as much damage as possible they would withdraw on the Manor House and the remainder of the Plan would be as in Defence Plan No.1'.[36]

If the tactics of the Home Guard were constantly under review, so was its organization. A further move to a more Army-type of administration was given in Army Council Instruction (ACI) 2100 of 27 October 1941. Battalions over 1,000 strong were now to have one Army officer (Adjutant / Quartermaster) together with one paid clerk and a storeman / clerk. It was noted in the instruction that units were often widely dispersed and that some officers also had civilian occupations. The need to encourage training required that correspondence should be kept to the minimum necessary for the training to be adequately carried out.[37] The Home Guard was now becoming a vast organisation based on Regular Army procedures. A 200-page book of regulations, excluding amendments, was now the Quartermaster's 'bible'. By October 1942 over 70 Army forms were in use. In addition, a plethora of Home Guard and Army Council Instructions, Home Guard Circulars, Command Orders, Regulations, and Daily Orders Parts 1 and 2 were being received. In addition, each platoon received over 100 different training handbooks during its life.[38]

Glyn Rowlands has described elements of the organization of the Shrewsbury Home Guard. His formation, the 1st Battalion, had its HQ at the Shropshire Yeomanry Riding School, the battalion's Adjutant and Quartermaster at the time Rowlands joined being Captain Howard, a

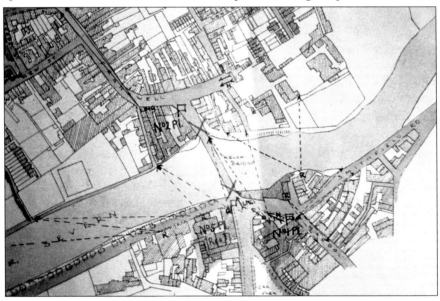

A 1944 defence plan for the Welsh Bridge in Shrewsbury from The Fighting Book of the Shropshire Home Guard. *Two platoon headquarters are located on either side of the river (numbers 1 and 2). This indicates the final and developed form of the town's defences and especially for an important point (a crossing of the Severn). A 2pdr anti-tank gun is located at the bottom of Mardol to fire towards the bridge which has anti-tank blocks at either end. Riflemen cover the river banks and the positions of Lewis guns are shown (LMG). A Northover Projector is positioned to fire along the flank into Frankwell. (Shropshire Archives)*

Regular Army officer seconded from the Herefordshire Light Infantry. (Glyn had joined at age 16 for which he needed his parents' written permission, but could not bear arms till he was 17). The battalion was divided into six companies, A to F. Each contained three platoons of up to 20 men in each. Rowlands' company, based at Coton Hill, was E, and covered Shelton Rough in the west to Hencote in the north-east. The company's commander was Major Makey who had served in the First World War and who was then the chief clerk of the Alliance Insurance Company in The Square. Their company sergeant-major was Jack Stone who lived at Greenfields and had been a regular in the KSLI. Rowlands' own platoon was based at Coton Hill Farm, which was also his home, the farm outbuildings being used to store ammunition and equipment. The platoon was commanded by Lieutenant Cole who had a painting and decorating business in Wyle Cop, whilst the second-in-command was Sergeant Jack North who lived on Swan Hill opposite the old County Police HQ. The Corporation Lane Section of the platoon had four reinforced trenches covering open ground to the north of the town, from the wood at Round Hill Green to the railway line at Coton Grange, the Great Western Railway line ran along the section's eastern boundary and their area also included the adjacent marshalling yards. Platoon parades were held at the West Midlands Showground each month when orders and other information were imparted.[39]

As the Home Guard became better armed and trained a more aggressive approach and role could be considered and this led to the formation of mobile columns, yet another change in tactics. A note from late 1941 records details of the Oswestry column: there was an HQ section, then a Reconnaissance section, a Rifle section, a Lewis gun section, and finally a Bomber section. Dedicated armament and equipment consisted of: 72 No.36 grenades, 72 No.69 grenades, eight 'Sticky Bombs' (see chapter 3), 12 anti-tank mines, 48 'molotoff bottles', eight smoke candles together with one coil of Dannert barbed wire (barbed wire in the form of a coil which could be extended concertina-like to form a barrier). To transport the column a four-seater car (for the HQ use) together with three lorries for the four sections were provided. All transport was of a civilian nature and requisitioned.[40]

As 1941 wore on and the threat of invasion once again seemed to diminish, the nature of the Home Guard was to undergo a major change, as it moved from a volunteer to a conscript force. In November, the National Service (No.2) Bill was introduced which contained provisions for the compulsory enrolment of men into the Civil Defence force and the Home Guard. The Ministry of Labour would decide on the manpower needs of each organization in an area so as to avoid imbalances where, for example, too many men in a particular area might otherwise join the Civil Defence force, with too few joining the Home Guard or *vice versa*. (The Civil Defence force had grown out of the pre-war Air Raid Precautions organisation into a large and complex body whose duties included warning the population of air raids; providing rescue and first-aid services after raids; decontaminating victims of gas attacks – something which fortunately never arose; and the welfare of casualties.) Conscripts had to be British subjects aged between 17 and 51. There could still be the voluntary enrolment of men aged between 17 and 65, of British or allied nationality or from a neutral state, but all now had to be of 'reasonable physical fitness'. Conscription brought in an element of compulsion concerning the attendance at parades, training events and exercises, and voluntary resignations were no longer permitted. 16-year-olds were allowed to join, but only as messengers.[41] Many older men now chose to resign, especially those aged over 65, although even after conscription was introduced certain men over this age were retained for short terms. Younger men who had resigned before conscription was brought in were often recalled after the introduction of the new system.

On 7 December 1941 Japanese forces attacked the US naval base at Pearl Harbour and Japan's ally Germany also declared war on the USA: America was now actively involved in the fighting.

In Home Guard Information Circular No.6 dated 20 December, the Director General and Staff of the War Office Home Guard Directorate was able to send to all members of the Home Guard 'All good wishes for Christmas and for 1942', whilst at the same time, in view of the need for economy, the circular requested that the sending of official Christmas cards 'was to be kept to a minimum'!

By the end of 1941 the Ellesmere Garrison, consisting of 120 men, armed with 90 rifles, six shotguns, five Lewis machine guns, two Browning machine guns and one Northover Projector (see chapter 3) could count itself fully equipped. Apart from covering their own localities there was only one official 'nodal point' defence position and this covered the Chirk bridge. Those situations when roadblocks were to be activated were given as: when there was enemy action outside the area; when there was enemy action on a large scale inside the area; and when the main operations were elsewhere but there were enemy parties within the units' areas. In the first situation the object was the checking of enemy agents, the checking being done by the police with the Home Guard providing escorts and defence. In the second situation the Chirk bridge post was to be manned by the Queenshead, Oswestry, and Ellesmere companies, the men having been issued with the necessary weapons, ammunition and with their anti-tank weapons sited.

Anti-tank hairpins would not be placed in position until the battalion was ordered to do so. Should a roadblock need to be opened, drivers would be ordered to dismount and to approach the post on foot for examination. If all was in order the occupants of the vehicles would be ordered to open the block (presumably this meant the moving of a light 'knife rest' wood and barbed wire obstacle), the last vehicle through closing the block with the Home Guard remaining under cover at all time.[42]

Where such blocks were intended to resist tank attack, detailed notes were given at a Sub Area lecture to the 2nd Battalion on 16 January 1942. Generally, all round defence was required with the sides of the roads and hedges flanking the roadblock to be covered in barbed wire. These blocks were to be sited on bends or in defiles so as to form an anti-tank obstruction. The system was:

1. Riflemen were to be stationed to prevent the removal of the block.
2. A bomb post was to be positioned to attack the enemy tanks.
3. A fougasse flame weapon (see chapter 3), if available, was to be placed ahead of the block.
4. A Northover Projector or Blacker Bombard (see chapter 3) was to be in the rear of the block.
5. An observation post was to give warning of an enemy's approach.
6. A get-away man was to be provided (presumably to warn other, adjacent Home Guard units, and/or summon support.)

At the same time the erection of improvised roadblocks was to cease as these were now considered to be quite valueless, leading to disruption with 'weakness everywhere and strength nowhere'.[43]

By early 1942 the role of the Home Guard was considered by Western Command in Instruction 958 as being the all round defence of selected localities, with the holding of strong or nodal points in depth, these being, if possible, mutually supporting. Concealment was essential. Local patrolling by day and night was to carry on and the Home Guard would be relied upon for the rapid transfer of information to the correct HQs. On the other hand, it was made clear that the Home Guard was not trained to conduct counterattacks.

Despite this, a somewhat contradictory, more aggressive role for the now better armed Home Guard was foreseen in the middle of 1942 by higher command. In July, the Chief of the General Staff GHQ Home Forces gave a press conference entitled 'If invasion comes' at which the position was summarised as follows:

The old LDV was formed after the invasion of the Low Countries primarily to counter the action of enemy parachutists. There were few trained troops in the country and practically no arms; the situation was very dangerous. Today things are different with properly trained and equipped military bodies who can attack enemy parachutists. The Home Guard has also developed, is now trained and equipped and now forms an essential part of the defence against invasion. The Home Guard is only equipped with light weapons and with no military transport or administration services so it is limited to its local area. However, this intimate knowledge of its own area gives it an advantage over the enemy.

Consider the problem facing Home Forces if an invasion is attempted:

1. The enemy will have the initiative and can concentrate his forces on the points he chooses along hundreds of miles of coast line.

2. He can attempt to land by air if he chooses.

3. We cannot have our troops everywhere so we must concentrate. But even if these are concentrated in the likely areas we would be strong nowhere and the enemy, by concentrating his attack, would always have the advantage. Our enemy would easily overcome local defence: we have little with which to stop him for all of our troops would be scattered where they would be of little value.

What we have to do is hold the beaches with mines, obstacles and guns and with the smallest number of men and keep as many mobile formations as possible in reserve for the counter-attack.

The enemy will succeed in getting ashore in places though we believe and are sure he will suffer heavy losses from air and naval action and land defences. Once ashore he must try to strike rapidly to his objective and this is when we counterattack and defeat him. To do this the enemy must be checked and disorganised to enable our reserves to arrive.

This is where the Home Guard comes into its own. Infantry and tanks can cross country but they cannot go far without their wheeled transport and this has to use roads, and these pass through towns and villages which can be made into excellent strong points. The main role allotted by the Commander in Chief is therefore the local defence of their own towns and villages. The Home Guard will not just engage in static defence but will also take mobile and aggressive action. Strong points are to be held with no withdrawal, but reserves are necessary to counterattack and harass if the opportunity arises, or to reinforce threatened localities. The Home Guard will play a most important role in winning the battle. Even if villages are bypassed by enemy armour, the action of the Home Guard in holding localities will cut off enemy troops from their [lorry-borne] ammunition supplies.

Other useful roles envisaged were: observation, information gathering by reconnaissance patrols, acting as guides for troops, the rounding up of parachutists in their areas, and traffic control. As a final observation it was said that:

> The role allotted to the Home Guard is one of the greatest tactical importance, suited to a force which is lightly armed and with little time for intensive training. It uses the stout hearts of the older members whilst giving scope for the initiative, enterprise and local knowledge of the younger members. To carry out this role really well all available time must be devoted to training for the actual operational task given. If invasion comes, it will be a grim battle against a ruthless enemy.[44]

Although the perceived threat from a fifth column had not gone away, by July 1942 a little more realism was creeping in and a Home Guard Instruction now admitted that:

> The publicity given by the press to enemy fifth column activities during the continental campaign resulted in a somewhat exaggerated view of the danger to this country. Excessive security etc against a possible fifth column might have the effect of hampering the mobility of regular forces. This danger was to be avoided as speed of movement and clear communications are essential in an invasion battle. Security must not be allowed to clog the military machine. But security mindedness is still necessary now or during an invasion, so 'suspicious alertness' must be cultivated by the Army and the Home Guard, so an enemy agent or fifth columnist cannot move for long without detection. Security is to be the servant and not the master of operations.[45]

Further reorganization of the Home Guard took place in 1942 with the formation of Invasion Committees. Generally, the functions of such committees included the co-ordination of civilian planning and the military scheme of defence: the enrolment of volunteers to dig trenches, the administration of first aid; the organisation of a messenger service; the provision of local sources of drinking water and the cooking and distribution of food; together with a census of tools and other items of use held in the town. One such committee was formed in Church Stretton. Here, plans for the defence of the local area were given at a committee meeting on 1 October 1942 with guidance from the official publication 'Consolidated Instructions to Invasion Committees'.

To the south of the town the valley had been barbed-wired and there were well-sited trenches, together with gun positions constructed to deny to the enemy the use of the roads. To the west of the town, it was reported that mobile Regular troops would occupy high points to prevent the enemy

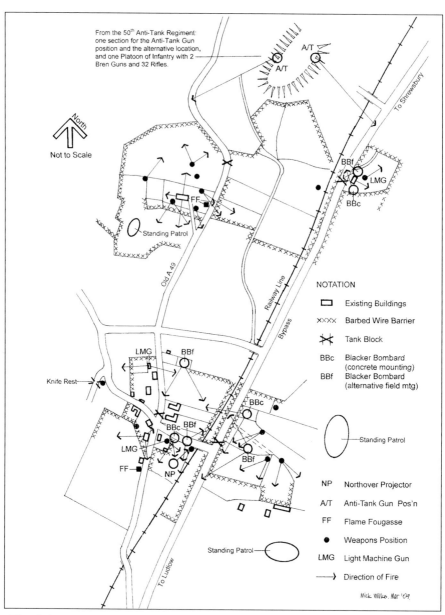

The defences of Little Stretton drawn from an undated Home Guard defence plan by Mick Wilks. The anti-tank positions at the top of the plan are located in the earthworks of a medieval castle and would probably have been manned by members of the 50th Anti-tank Regiment who were stationed in the vicinity until August 1943. Part of the defence scheme included the use of the flame fougasse weapon sniping at and outflanking the outer defences. To the east, a defended locality had been established and provided with well-sited trenches. To the north, a defended locality had been reconnoitred. (The town sat on the main A49 road in a strategic position with approaches from the west blocked by the Long Mynd which had itself been protected against enemy airborne attack by the presence of the 50th Anti Tank Training Regiment, whose presence also boosted the town's defences until their departure in August 1943). Approaches from the east were also difficult due to the hilly nature of the country. Although a bypass had been constructed at the outbreak of war this had been taken over as a military vehicle park, as had the Shrewsbury bypass.

The Committee was informed of a number of roadblocks: one lay on the bypass south of the Laundry and near a high concrete wall, one was north of the hotel (presumably the Long Mynd Hotel); one was to its east; one lay north of the Gas Works, and one was on the old road, on the corner north of Little Stretton.

Drawings of emergency trenches and latrines (including 'temporary pail closets') were produced for the committee, the former providing shelter and the latter a little comfort for the embattled population during an invasion.[46]

The activities of the Home Guard were further developed in 1943. Details survive of the role that A Company of the 2nd Battalion, which covered the Ellesmere area, would have played. Broadly, the company would have supplied a garrison for nodal point defences along with patrols covering the company's area. The aim was to deny the enemy the use of road communications and the resources of the town. The scale of any attack was now considered likely to consist of small airborne enemy operations, which would attempt to sabotage factories, supplies and communications; and/or enemy columns which had broken through from the main battle area endeavouring to harass local lines of communications, probably accompanied by armoured vehicles. Roadblocks would be manned, but the bulk of the force would be kept in reserve for offensive action or to occupy its defensive positions. To carry out this role the company had eight platoons: three in Ellesmere plus five others based at Plas yn Grove, Welsh Frankton, Lee plus Hordley, and Welshampton, with the final platoon being formed of men working at the RAOC depot at Elson.

On the issue of the code word OLIVER ('invasion has occurred and the enemy is in the vicinity') a number of defensive dispositions were to be taken in the parish churchyard, Scotland Street and Grange Road areas. The vulnerable points of the telephone exchange, electricity transformers, the milk factory, gas works and the police station were to be protected. In

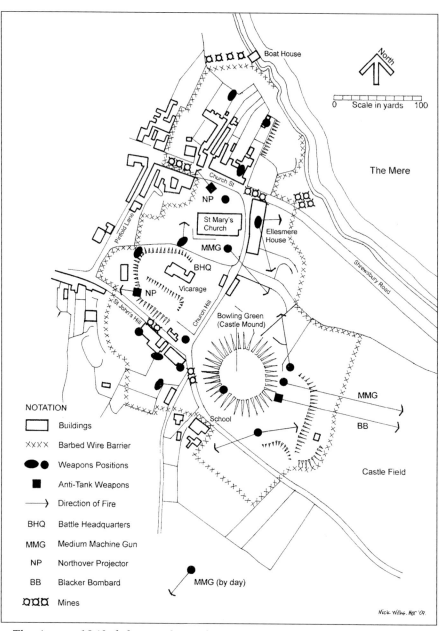

Boat House

North

Scale in yards
0   100

The Mere

Church St

NP

St Mary's
Church

Ellesmere
House

Pinfold Lane

MMG

BHQ

Vicarage

NP

St John's Hill

Church Hill

Bowling Green
(Castle Mound)

Shrewsbury Road

MMG

School

BB

Castle Field

NOTATION

▭	Buildings
✕✕✕	Barbed Wire Barrier
⬤⬤	Weapons Positions
◼	Anti-Tank Weapons
⟶	Direction of Fire
BHQ	Battle Headquarters
MMG	Medium Machine Gun
NP	Northover Projector
BB	Blacker Bombard
◻◻◻	Mines

MMG (by day)

Nick Wilks. Mar '09.

*The August 1943 defence scheme for Ellesmere from a Home Guard plan
drawn by Mick Wilks. The steel rail defences of the town are not marked
although the location of minefields are marked. The Blacker Bombard
(29mm Spigot Mortar) by the castle appears to be in an unusual position as
it is not associated with a nearby anti-tank block*

48

the church area were five roadblocks including ones at St John's Hill (with a Blacker Bombard) and Church Hill where there was a single row of steel girders. In the Scotland Street sector were three roadblocks, one of which had a Blacker Bombard. The Grange Road sector also had three roadblocks, one consisting of mines only, one with a Blacker Bombard and the third with a screen '100 yards NW of the crossroads'. Presumably this was to confuse an enemy as to what lay beyond the screen and, hopefully, delay them!

These dispositions were intended to meet a 'serious enemy threat against the town and neighbourhood'. A series of defended platoon localities were to be held on the perimeter of Ellesmere, with an inner keep in Watergate Street. Each locality was organised for all round defence. Sub-sector reserves were intended to occupy additional localities in order to strengthen the existing ones or to counter an enemy counterattack. Ammunition and emergency rations were to be held at the Company HQ, first aid was to be provided at Trimpley Hall, and there would be food cooking centres established. Emergency communications were to be provided by a runner or a despatch rider. All of the positions were to be held 'to the last man and the last round'.[47]

With the prospect of an invasion gradually diminishing, keeping up the motivation of the Home Guard was becoming a challenge. On 31 May 1943 Colonel Morris Eyton wrote to the commander of A Company:

> I am convinced that the Home Guard is entering a very diffi-
> cult period as there are currents of a feeling that the 'war is over'.
> Excessive writing-up of the Tunisian campaign where only 2% of
> the German army was defeated is largely responsible. The UK is not
> a military minded nation and we have no clear idea of the total size
> and strength of the German army. It is essential to keep Companies in
> being, but any attempt to force excessive training will fail. Company
> commanders are to consider giving harvest leave and reducing parade
> hours, giving the impression this is due to the (improved) military
> situation.

The recipient also made his feelings clear as he wrote a note in red pencil on the message: 'Any relaxation in the matter of prosecutions will <u>add</u> to the cross-currents! Essential to give generous harvest leave. Best to give in and go the other way. Organise harvesting parties of Ministry of Agricultural workers and offer them to farmers. If necessary make them parade'.[48]

With the success of the Normandy landings in June 1944 and the Soviets' victories on the Eastern Front it was clear that the days of the Home Guard were numbered. Shortly after D-Day an Army memo marked 'Secret' was issued on 24 July 1944 and received by the Adjutant of the 2nd Battalion at Walford Manor, the subject being 'Road Blocks', to the effect that all steel rails for roadblocks and anti-tank obstacles were to be piled in the HQ car park. A circular six days previously had already instructed that all steel rails as erected were to be withdrawn and disposed of as salvage. The given reason was 'on account of the steel shortage and no modification of the existing policy of defended localities was entailed'. Concrete blocks and cylinders were not yet to be removed. Should some alteration in the future situation occur in the manning of defended localities, battalion commanders were to augment the existing concrete road blocks with such additional obstacles as could be improvised locally, stiffening these with No.75 (Hawkins) grenades and covering blocks with 2pdr anti-tank guns as far as possible, together with any other equipment which would be used in that role.

On 14 September 1944 a further instruction regarding roadblocks and obstacles was issued to the HQ of the 2nd Battalion (and copied to all companies including that at Ellesmere), to the effect that it was no longer necessary to retain roadblocks or obstacles on highways and therefore these would be dismantled or demolished when the necessary labour became available. The greatest priority was to be given to the removal of obstacles to traffic.[49]

An earlier Western Command Instruction (No.460) of May 1944 had warned of the danger to the public caused by the non-replacement of socket covers and the faulty stacking of steel rails, so one imagines the public were glad to see the gradual removal of the paraphernalia of home defence. The steel rails were intended to be recycled for the war effort, whilst it seems that the county council had the responsibility of disposing of the concrete cubes and cylinders. It is known that many were dumped in one of the quarries at Grinshill whilst others were used to revet the banks of the Severn at Bridgnorth. Others can still be seen at various locations about the county.[50]

With the success of the allies and the gradual dismantling of home defences, the days of the Home Guard were limited. On 1 November 1944 the order came to stand down the organisation. Local parades were held on Sunday 3 December, a wet day, by each battalion. A grand parade was also held in London that day, the county being represented by Lieutenant Hunt of the 5th Battalion plus three other ranks from each of the other battalions. At stand down the county's combined strength had been 15,107 men including 903 officers, but the total number of men who had served for varying periods was 31,110, many passing into the Regular Army or

Men of the Bridgnorth Home Guard get ready to take part in the stand down parade held on Sunday 3 December. As can be seen it was a wet and gloomy day

into industry in other parts of country. Many women from the county had provided vital support as Home Guard Women Auxiliaries whilst not having to bear arms or wear a uniform. Although the organisation was officially finished, units were encouraged to turn themselves into rifle clubs or old comrades associations.

For some time after the end of the war ceremonies were held to celebrate the anniversary of the formation of the force. And it has been said that no spectator failed to be impressed by the bearing and training of the members of the force during its life.[51] It had also been a remarkably cheap army: in December 1944 it was calculated that its total cost had been £1.8m, or less than £9 per enrolled man! In the opinion of one officer in the Shropshire Home Guard this may have been because the Territorial Army Association 'never spent any money and personal equipment was always short' and he felt that there was a general 'lack of effort by the TAA'. One member of his company, Lieutenant Owen, had been waiting for a greatcoat that would fit him and four measurements had been submitted without success: it hadn't arrived by the time the force was stood down! The officer also felt that Regular Army Adjutants didn't appreciate that many members of the Home Guard also worked, and that conscription had been a mistake with only 20% of those conscripted being any good.[52]

Looking back to the early days of the organisation, an unnamed officer of the Shropshire Home Guard, formerly the second-in-command of the Harrogate Battalion before taking up a fulltime position as the Administration Assistant at the Shropshire Zone HQ in Shrewsbury in August 1940, recalled the organization's early days. He felt that Anthony Eden's broadcast had had the strongest response from First World War ex-servicemen as they believed that, in the event of fighting taking place, this was best done by those with previous military experience. However, at the time of this recollection in 1943, after the introduction of conscription, men with such experience were few and far between, in part a recognition of their increasing age and in part due to the demands of fitness and stamina required even for Home Guard duties. But he felt the loss of these older men was a sad business following conscription and the introduction of an upper age limit of 65, as many of the veterans had 'worked to the bone' in the first year of the organisation's life. On the other hand, some veterans had also felt that, after fighting on the Western Front in the First World War, they could hardly believe that they would now be expected to man flimsy last ditch defences for as long as their ammunition held.[53]

By a quirk of history, and shortly before the Home Guard was stood down, Germany was creating a similar body, the Volkssturm. This had also had to begin by wearing what uniforms were available in 1944 and by being armed with whatever weapons were to hand. Initially, their duties were similar to those of the Home Guard: the tracking down and elimination of enemy agents and saboteurs, the protection of bridges and other vulnerable points, the guarding of prisoners of war and the filling of breaches in regular army formations. Many fought bravely, suffering appalling casualties on the eastern frontiers of the Reich, but on the western front most were happy to give little resistance to the advancing British and US forces.

A fitting postscript to life in the Home Guard can be found in the letter from Morris Eyton to the commander of D Company of the 2nd Battalion at stand down:

> Dear Major Jones,
> It was most kind of you and your officers to send me the autographed history of D Company. It will be a very much valued keepsake of our

happy association with the Home Guard and I hope when they get a bit older the children will get to value it too, and be a spur to them to serve their country as so many good fellows whose names are therein have done in their time. We have been a very happy family and have found much contentment in our service. Very many thanks to you all.

C.R. Morris Eyton.[54]

There was, however, a price to pay and a number of men lost their lives in service. Details, where known, are given below of those who died:

William John Sydney Biddulph of the 1st Battalion was killed on 6 October 1941 aged 61 and was buried at Perry Barr cemetery, Birmingham.

Lt Reginald Eustace Massey of the 7th Battalion, Clee Hill Company, collapsed and died aged 43 whilst engaged in a training exercise on 20 June 1943. He is buried at Bitterly.

Lt Frank Cyril Hopwood of the 7th Battalion was shot and fatally wounded during a Sten gun demonstration, aged 46, on 24 May 1942 and is buried at Clun.

Walter Goddard of the 2nd Battalion died on 21 September 1941 aged 64 and was cremated in Manchester.

Private J. Woolley, believed to have been attached as a despatch rider to the 1st Battalion HQ, died on 19 July 1944 when his motorcycle collided with a lorry.[55]

If it was thought that the end of the Second World War marked the end of the organisation, there was a surprise in store a few years later. The Soviet blockade of Berlin in 1948 and the realisation of the threat from the Soviet Union and the possibility of politically motivated civilian unrest set in motion a plan for the re-formation of the Home Guard. The new force was formed by the passing of the Home Guard Act of 1951 but countrywide recruiting was painfully slow. In Shropshire the new force had, again, its Administrative HQ in Shrewsbury and five Battalions were raised under the leadership of Colonel J.N. Ritchie. These remained active until 1957. They were the 1st Battalion (Shrewsbury), the 2nd Battalion (Wrekin and Wellington), the 3rd Battalion (Oswestry), the 4th Battalion (East Broseley) and the 5th Battalion (Craven Arms). The county organisation was affiliated to the 4th Battalion (TA) KSLI, the commanders being Lt Col Morgan, Lt Col Lanyon, Lt Col Faithful, Lt Col the Lord Forester and Lt Col Coldwell. In 1956, due to the general lack of enthusiasm for the new force and changing military tactics, it was decided to disband the force from 31 July

1957. It had not achieved the popularity of the Second World War force and had struggled to recruit meaningful numbers of men, let alone its country-wide target strength of 125,000.[56]

Chapter 3

Arming the Shropshire Home Guard

When the Local Defence Volunteers was established in Shropshire it appears to have been largely reliant on publicly donated shotguns. In June 1940, precedence had to be given to rearming the Army after the disastrous losses of equipment following the withdrawal of the British Expeditionary Force from France. The situation for the LDV, even in Kent which would have borne the brunt of the German invasion, was dire. Despite over 10,000 men joining the LDV on the first 24 hours in Kent, by the middle of May only 3,500 Army rifles had been issued.[1] This would only change in late summer with the arrival of US P17 rifles. Away from the invasion coast, the arms issued in the early days of the LDV were even more sparse.

Because its rifles and machine guns eventually came from US stocks, the Home Guard used the US .30 calibre round rather than the Army's .303 calibre round. This minuscule difference was sufficient to prevent the inter-changeability of ammunition, however. Although the weapons came with some ammunition from the USA, the Home Guard had to wait for the UK manufacture of its ammunition to catch up with demand at a time when the Army was also short of stocks of ammunition. Any .303 weapons received by the Home Guard in 1940 such as the British Lee-Enfield or Canadian Ross .303 rifles or the .303 Lewis gun were passed back to Army stores, with the latter weapon being passed on to RAF which, like the Army, used this calibre. Gradually the Home Guard was supplied with other weapons so that, by September 1942, they had effective short range anti-tank weapons (mines and the Northover Projector, Smith Gun and Spigot Mortar) as well as grenades, medium and light machine guns, submachine guns as well as rifles. This was a vast if slow improvement over the position in June 1940.[2]

The Shotgun

This was often the only weapon available in the early days of the LDV and Home Guard. In May 1940 one company in the 2nd Battalion had 'thirty to forty' shotguns, mostly loaned, together with three First World War vintage revolvers. (In contrast, four years later, the same company had 94 .30 rifles, 10 EY rifles (see below), 5 Vickers .30 machine guns, 6 Lewis guns, 1 Spigot Mortar, 44 Sten submachine guns and 4 revolvers.) The shotguns were later returned to their owners.[3] This weapon was not totally ineffectual as an infantry weapon and it is believed that some shotguns remained in use until the Home Guard was stood down: it would have proved a devastating weapon at close range. Over 2,000 were willingly lent in Shropshire. Special ball ammunition which had been 'exhaustively tested' was issued. This was considered safe for most shotguns except, for example, very old damascened barrels and especially those manufactured 'before the advent of nitro powder'.

The commanding officer of the 2nd Battalion wrote on 29 May 1940 optimistically forecasting that 'sufficient rifles should be forthcoming to arm all men efficient in their use', although 'men proficient with the shotgun but not rifle should be armed with the former'. He added however, that if sufficient rifles did not materialise 'then shotguns will be added'.[4] How these weapons might come into the possession of the LDV is indicated by a memo dated 5 October 1940 from C Company of the 3rd Battalion. On 4 July the local police had, apparently, visited local gunshops and seized shotguns and cartridges which were handed to the LDV. All the cartridges, with the exception of two boxes which couldn't be traced, were returned to the police two days later, the shotguns being issued to the company's 2nd Platoon. In October the company had had a visit from the police asking who was to pay the tradesman for the two guns still held by the 2nd Platoon and for the unreturned cartridges. The Commander of C Company's memo stated that 'I expect we shall have to pay for the cartridges', whilst asking the police 'on whose orders the shotguns were dumped on this company'.[5]

Rifles

Before the general issue of US P17 rifles, a relatively small number of First World War era .303 Lee-Enfield and Canadian Ross rifles had been distributed to the Shropshire Home Guard. These were returned to Army stores as P17s became available so that a common calibre (.30) prevailed for their use.

The genesis of the Home Guard's mainstay P17 rifle is as follows. US manufacturers in The First World War had been contracted to manufacture

Members of the Wheathill Home Guard. The rear row of men hold P17 rifles. The officer in the centre has a leather case for his pistol or revolver and he is flanked by men armed with Sten guns and one who holds a Lewis light machine gun. (Shropshire Archives)

the Enfield-designed .303 Pattern 1914 rifle for the British Army. As the war was coming to an end the various contractors carried on manufacturing the gun for the US Army, but adapting it to the US .30 calibre, this weapon to be known as the M1917 rifle, usually referred to as the P(attern) 17 in Home Guard service. Over one million were supplied from the late summer of 1940. To indicate the use of the .30 round instead of .303, red bands were painted around the front and rear portions of each rifle. It was a rather clumsy but accurate weapon. Like the Wehrmacht's Mauser rifle it had a magazine holding five rounds as opposed to the British Army's Lee-Enfield .303 rifle which held ten rounds.

Despite the wait for these weapons it seems that not all members of the Home Guard treated their prized rifle well: Home Guard Instruction No.48 of July 1942 noted that the rifle was not always respected. On exercises there were cases noted of rifles being thrown out of lorries or being used for assisting climbing. Culprits were to be admonished: 'A damaged rifle risks being inaccurate, leading to the loss of the owner's life'. The rifle was no longer a 'personal defensive weapon' as mentioned in earlier training manuals, but was now an 'offensive killing weapon'. The instruction went on to say, optimistically, that 'small arms fire against tanks is often successful in smashing [and therefore blinding] periscopes on tanks' and 'all Home Guard who are attacking tanks are to bear this in mind'.[6]

Morris Eyton warned all 2nd Battalion members of the threat of the theft of

Men of the Eaton Constantine Home Guard pose after a church parade. Of interest is the fact that they have the cumbersome bayonets for the P17 rifle slung from their leather belts. Most if not all carry the military respirator case slung over their shoulders. The impractical field service cap has the badge of the parent army regiment (KSLI) pinned to it

rifles in a circular dated 16 August 1941. Apparently one battalion in the county had lost 16 rifles that had been stolen in a 'novel [but unspecified] way'. In another instance two men had gone to the house of a member of the Home Guard whilst he was at work, saying to his wife that they had been sent by his battalion to collect his rifle.[7] Theft might have been a comparatively simple affair as some members were lax in their security measures. John Hughes's brother, Wilfred Hughes, had joined A Company of the Shrewsbury Home Guard aged 16½. He remembers Wilfred having a Browning automatic rifle and also a Lewis light machine gun which he was in the habit of leaving on his mother's sideboard.[8]

The 'EY' rifle

The P17 was also the basis for a type of crude personal mortar known as the 'EY rifle' (apparently after the initials of its inventor Edgar Youle), also known as the 'DC' (Discharger Cup). The barrel was strengthened with a wire binding to withstand the pressures of the special 'ballistite' cartridge that projected the missile, usually the No.36M grenade. The weapon was fired with its butt on the ground and at a 45 degree angle, the operator adopting a kneeling position.

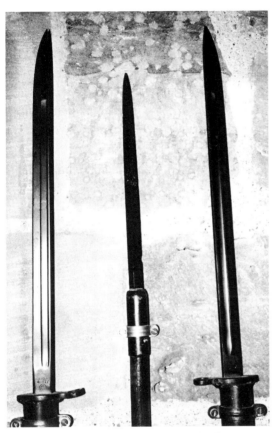

The infamous Home Guard pike: these examples are in the Shropshire Regimental Museum

Pikes

A medieval touch was added with the issue to the Home Guard of the notorious pike. This was not a desperate measure of 1940 but emanated from an idea of Churchill's. Towards the end of June 1941 Churchill, perhaps on hearing that not all members of the rapidly expanding force were armed, was moved to write to the War Office that 'every man must have a weapon of some kind even if a mace or a pike'. The War Office took the instruction literally and ordered truncheons and a quarter of a million pikes to be made from obsolete bayonets rammed into steel tubes.[9] Although it is unlikely that many were actually issued to members of the Home Guard, a memo of March 1942 from the Bishops Castle Home Guard mentions the existence of two pikes and ten truncheons, whilst from Plowden Hall (7th Battalion) a register of kit included ten rubber truncheons and 'two bayonets on sticks'. However, these latter had not actually been issued to members of the force.[10] Examples of the pike can be seen in the Shropshire Regimental Museum.

The Thompson submachine gun

The Home Guard also received numbers of the famous Thompson .45 calibre submachine gun, more famously known as the 'Tommy Gun', in 1940. This

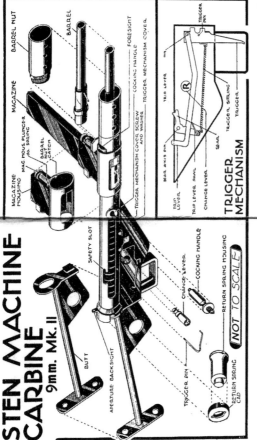

STEN MACHINE CARBINE
9mm. Mk. II

THE STEN MACHINE CARBINE Mk. II, 9mm.

The Home Guard will realise that its fire power has been considerably increased by the introduction of this, its latest weapon.

The most effective use of the Sten Carbine can only be secured by constant handling. This applies to the operation of the cocking handle and change lever, charging and changing magazines and unloading, and also the quick and automatic alignment of sights from the shoulder and from the hip. A firm grip with both hands is essential.

Waste no time—read the following and become familiar with the construction, handling, care and uses of the Sten.

BRIEF DESCRIPTION

THE STEN MACHINE CARBINE Mk. II, 9mm. will fire all types of 9mm. round nose rimless ammunition. Some Machine Carbines of the German Army also use this type of ammunition. Operation is by blowback and return spring. Firing may be "Automatic" (in bursts) or "Single Shots." Carbine should be fired dry and thoroughly clean. Barrel and Butt are easily detachable to facilitate carriage. Fixed sights for use up to 200 yds.

		lb	oz.
WEIGHT	Carbine, assembled, without magazine	6	10
	Magazine (empty)	—	10
	Magazine, filled, 32 rounds	1	7
LENGTH	Carbine, assembled		30″
	Barrel		7·8″
	Body		13″
	Butt		10·5″
	Magazine		9·5″

RATE OF FIRE Cyclic — 500–550

SIGHTS Aperture backsight and inverted "V" foresight.

RIFLING Barrel is rifled, six grooves, right-hand.

MAGAZINE Box type, Mark II, 32-round capacity. Magazine is inserted in Housing on left side and retained by spring-loaded catch.

STRIPPING

See that Carbine is unloaded and **Breech Block forward.**

BUTT—Press in Return Spring Housing and slide Butt down.

BREECH BLOCK—Press forward Return Spring Cap and Housing about quarter of an inch and rotate about one-eighth turn anti-clockwise, thus disengaging the Cap lugs from their slots in the casing. Remove Housing, Cap and Spring. Draw Breech Block backward and remove Cocking Handle when opposite Safety Slot. Place Cocking Handle in front of Breech Block, draw back and clear.

BARREL—Disengage Barrel Nut Catch, rotate Magazine Housing, anti-clockwise. Unscrew Barrel Nut and remove with Barrel.

TRIGGER MECHANISM

TRIGGER MECHANISM—Turn Carbine upside down:

1 Remove Screw and Washer on each side, lift Cover.
2 Unhook Trigger Spring from Trip Lever Pawl and Trigger.
3 Remove Trip Lever Pawl.
4 Push out Sear Axis Pin and remove Sear.
5 Draw out Change Lever Split Pin and, while holding Trip Lever clear, remove Change Lever.

A Gale and Polden leaflet explaining the workings of the Sten gun.

This is an example of one of the many privately-produced manuals for purchase by the Home Guard automatic weapon came with 20 or 30 round box magazines or a circular 50 round magazine. How numerous this heavy but well-made weapon was in Shropshire is not known. It is likely that some were in service as on 24 March 1942 the county Territorial Army Association wrote to Colonel Morris Eyton of the 2nd Battalion (and presumably to other Battalions) that 'Sten submachine guns are to be issued in exchange for the Thompson. The first consignment of Stens will shortly be available. The Thompson is required by the War Office for service elsewhere.'[11]

The Sten gun

It was intended that the Thompson's successor, the new 9mm Sten submachine gun, was to be issued with a technical booklet, but as an emergency measure a pamphlet was issued whilst the booklet was pending. Again, this was an automatic weapon with a 32 round box magazine. As usual, little ammunition was initially available, only 20 rounds per gun and these were to be used for proving. Easily and cheaply made, it suffered from various weaknesses. For example, if the butt was knocked the gun could fire even if uncocked, this being due to its weak recoil spring which could be driven back and then forward to start the firing cycle.

The Browning Automatic Rifle

This had a 20 round magazine underneath the gun. Although it could be used on automatic fire mode like a light machine gun, single shot fire was specified for Home Guard use as automatic fire was considered wasteful of ammunition. Indeed the weapon had not been designed as a light machine gun: it was not steady enough for this role and was, generally, a rather heavy if sturdy weapon for infantry use. The weapon formed a component part of Home Guard Battle Squads.

Vickers and Browning machine guns

Although some units in the county received examples of the .30 Vickers air cooled machine gun (possibly, again, an ex aircraft gun from US stocks), it seems that the water-cooled US Browning M1917 .30 infantry machine gun was the most numerous heavy machine gun in Home Guard use. Like the Vickers, this weapon was belt fed, and was generally similar in appearance to the Army's Vickers .303 machine gun. The weapon, because of its weight, had to be broken down into sections or transported on trailers and was only used as a defensive weapon.

Lewis light machine gun

Referred to as the 'LMG' by the Home Guard, the Lewis gun had been adopted by the British army in the First World War. Examples of this weapon seen in use by the Home Guard lack the outer cooling jacket of the Army's weapons and were probably ex-aircraft weapons of .30 calibre and from US stocks. It was fitted with a circular drum magazine. The gun, fitted with a crude bipod and shoulder stock for ground use, provided the Home Guard with a light machine gun capability for both ground and anti-aircraft use. The Home Guard, generally speaking, was not issued with the British Army's Bren light machine gun. The Lewis was not considered to be wholly reliable, however, being prone to many different types of feed stoppages.

The advent of such automatic weapons was often not wholly appreciated by members of the Home Guard, despite their clamour for extra firepower. In October 1941 it was noted that Lewis guns were suffering from excessive stripping and that their sights were often damaged or out of alignment. These

The military identity card of Lieutenant Harold Moulton
of the 7th Battalion. He was an ammunition officer, checking on the safety of
the stockpiles of ammunition and explosives held by his battalion.
As the landlord of the Salway Arms Hotel (south of Ludlow on the A49)
he was given the nickname of 'Doctor' on account of the 'remedies' that he
dispensed to members of the battalion at his establishment

criticisms also applied to the Thompson. As for the Browning machine gun, 'maintenance leaves much to be desired. Dirt was often present, there was a lack of adequate lubrication, and rough and ready re-assembly after stripping was often noted.'[12] In future, this memo stated, 'no stripping was to take place unless by an authorised armourer, and all guns in future were to be kept oiled and in a clean condition'.

Grenades

In common with the British Army, the Home Guard used the reliable No.36M anti-personnel fragmentation hand grenade, also known as the 'Mills Bomb'. This could be thrown by hand, projected using the 'DC' / 'EY' rifle or by firing it from the Northover Projector. Another hand grenade used was the No.69 Grenade, made of Bakelite and relying on blast for its effect.

The desperate need for an anti-tank weapon saw the manufacture in 1940 of thousands of Molotov Cocktails for the Home Guard and the Army. The name is believed to have been bestowed by the Finnish army during that country's war with the USSR in 1939-40: Molotov was the Soviet Foreign Minister. It was also used with some success in the Spanish Civil War. The weapon was thrown in the hope that the burning mixture would blind an enemy tank's vision ports or, if sufficient hit the engine vents on the rear of the tank, to ignite oil and fuel in the engine compartment. Instructions issued in the summer of 1940 advised the use of empty beer or whisky bottles filled with a mixture of two parts petrol, one part paraffin and one part liquid tar. Six hits might stop a tank, causing the crew to evacuate. They were manufactured locally, the petrol and special matches being supplied by the military.[13] Ignition of the mixture was by an attached, petrol soaked rag or by two *fusée* slow burning matches attached to the bottle's side. Contemporary training notes describe the right type of man for the job of throwing the bomb as one with a 'cool, fearless and adventurous disposition'![14] A more sophisticated version of the Molotov Cocktail was known as the SIP, AW Bomb or No.77 grenade. SIP stood for Self-Igniting Phosphorous and AW referred to the manufacturer, Albright and Wilson of Oldbury, Worcestershire. The incendiary mixture was held in a glass bottle, and a piece of rubber was introduced to the mixture to make the benzene mixture stick: phosphorous stabilised in water ignited the benzene and rubber on contact with air, as when the glass container broke against the side of a tank. This weapon, like the No.36M grenade, could also be fired from the Northover Projector or could be thrown by hand from 'bombing pits' adjacent to anti-tank roadblocks.

The No.73 grenade, also called the 'Thermos Flask Grenade', contained a high explosive charge and was designed as an anti-tank weapon. This weapon was quickly dropped from operational use, one shortcoming being that it was vulnerable to small arms fire, but it served as a source of explosive and detonators for demolition work.

A more effective anti-tank grenade was the No.75 Hawkins or 'Talcum Powder Bomb' — so named because its case resembled a talcum powder tin. It was cheap to make but effective, and was designed to withstand a weight of 2cwt before exploding. The explosion of one grenade was said to be capable of snapping the track of a German Mk IV tank: two would do the same but also blow off a bogey wheel.[15] It was therefore also useful as a demolition charge on railways.

The No.74 ST or 'Sticky bomb' had, like the Nos.73, 77 and Molotov Cocktail weapons, the need for the thrower to get close to an enemy tank. The drawback of this weapon was that its sticky coating often stuck better to a battledress than a wet and muddy Panzer tank! The Home Guard was also issued with the No.77 white phosphorous smoke grenade. A Western Command circular issued to the Home Guard in October 1944 instructed that farmers were to be warned not to graze their stock over ground contaminated by white phosphorous for a period of fourteen days.[16]

Also issued were the large Army anti-tank mines. There are several references in Home Guard papers to these: a Junior Leaders Course held at Ludlow in late 1940 gave instructions in their use and the 7th Battalion Defence Scheme of December 1941 refers to them. A map of the defences of Ellesmere, specially redrawn for this book by Mick Wilks (see p.48), shows the location of 'mine pots', sockets made in road surfaces ready to take a mine. These also formed a component of the defences of Ludlow and Shrewsbury, sockets being located in the latter, for example, by the Sutton Road and Abbey Foregate railway bridges.[17] Home Guard Instruction 48 of July 1942 stated 'contrary to instructions, Marks II, IV and V mines are to be buried with their tops not more than half an inch below the surface'.

Sub Artillery

Northover Projector
This was a smoothbore weapon, consisting of a long barrel mounted on a stand, firing the No. 68 anti-tank, No. 76 SIP or No. 36M grenades, these being projected by the ignition of a charge of gunpowder. It was designed as a light, short range ambush weapon with a range of about 120 yards. With this weapon, however, there was always the risk of the gunpowder charge firing incorrectly leading to 'shorts', that is, the grenade landing too close to the operators of the weapon.

A modern replica of the Northover Projector with, on the left, the wooden carrying case for No.76 (SIP) grenades

29 mm Spigot Mortar
(also known as the Blacker Bombard after its inventor)

Like the Northover Projector this was another emergency weapon, originally conceived for use by regular forces from 1941 onwards to make up for the Army's catastrophic loss of light artillery at Dunkirk in 1940. Initially it was intended for use as a light coastal defence weapon or for the defence of airfields. The RAF soon stopped using the weapon, but the Army used it in North Africa briefly before passing it on to the Home Guard who at least appreciated some form of anti-tank artillery with a secondary anti-personnel capability. With a 20lb anti-tank bomb it had a maximum range of 200 yards. Home Guard

A surviving Spigot Mortar position which must have been used for training attendees at the No.3 GHQ Home Guard Training School at Stokesay Court. Originally in a former quarry it is now within an SSSI at View Edge, one mile north-west of the school

A 29mm Spigot Mortar ('Blacker Bombard') being demonstrated to HRH George VI in Hyde Park, London. Typically it is sited in a circular trench with the weapon pivoting on a steel pin set into the concrete 'thimble'. Inert practice rounds lie on the rim of the trench. These were placed in the large barrel and the weapon was moved using the two handles to the right of the shield

Instruction No.48 of July 1942 described the device as an 'ambush weapon that was not to be converted into a mobile weapon by adding wheels'. Each weapon was provided with one portable mounting and up to four, alternative, fixed pedestal positions which were said to give more accurate fire. Wherever possible these were set in pits. This heavy weapon was optimistically said to be capable of being moved 'rapidly to alternative positions if necessary', and all crews were asked to learn how to use both mountings.

Not all of the Home Guard unreservedly welcomed the new weapon. Colonel Morris Eyton, following its introduction in 1942, was 'not at first struck with the usefulness of the Blacker Bombard in this strong point [Montford Bridge] as an ambush is out of the question and its range is short'. Another disadvantage was that its bombs were, like the Northover Projector, projected by black powder and not by smokeless powder and camouflage was essential. Realistically it was a 'one shot' weapon.[18] However, many Spigot Mortars were emplaced in the county with Ellesmere and Shrewsbury, for example, being ringed by fixed positions.[19]

One document records what happened to such positions when they were no longer required. On 9 October 1944 the War Department land agent and valuer in Shrewsbury wrote to the Reverend Moir at Bromfield Vicarage informing him that a Spigot Mortar on church land 'may be dismantled' but that there were 'no troops available to remove [it]' and the 'onus was on the owner of the land to do the work. From recent inspections of similar works, removal does not present a problem. Many farmers were willing to clear such sites, making no claim for compensation', although the Reverend Moir was to '… advise if compensation was to be sought.' After further correspondence the War Department Valuer wrote to the Reverend Moir on 11 November 1944 saying that in fact the only way to remove the Spigot Mortar pedestal appeared to be to blow it up or have it buried. According to a letter from the War Department dated 22 January 1945 it appears that in the event the trenches and mounting were dismantled by the local garrison engineer and no compensation was sought.[20]

The 'Smith Gun'
(officially known as the 3 inch Ordnance Smooth Bore)

To what extent this ungainly weapon was used in Shropshire is not fully known, as it was 'only issued on a limited scale where operationally required'. An undated plan of the defences of the 6th Battalion in the Madeley, Coalbrookdale and Ironbridge does, however, record a 'Smith Gun Battery' on the south-eastern outskirts of Madeley.[21] In addition, the *Fighting Book of 1st Battalion Salop Home Guard* (see below) records eight of these weapons in its charge in July 1944.

The weapon was moved on large and narrow wheels, one of which, when the weapon was tipped over into the firing position, provided overhead cover for the gun crew. It easily became bogged down on rough ground but in theory could be used for house to house fighting, the recommendation being that it be moved by younger Home Guard with the aid of toggle ropes. The weapon's range was 200 yards and a limber carried both anti-tank and high explosive rounds. Advice issued included that 'It has some mobility and the crews should be selected from reasonably agile men in the offensive/ defensive sub-units. At least two crews of four men are to be trained. The less agile Home Guard members should be detailed and trained as crews for the Northover Projector which remains one of the most effective short range ambush Home Guard weapons'. A memo in June 1943 reported on the cartridges for the Smith Gun: there had been 'unfortunate accidents due to early batches of ammunition' giving the weapon a 'reputation for lack of safety and inefficiency', but these were 'just temporary troubles concerning the fusing of the ammunition' for there had been the 'successful firing of 1,000 rounds'.[22]

Flame Weapons

The Home Guard relied upon a number of flame weapons, including the already mentioned Molotov Cocktail and SIP grenades. Another weapon was the Harvey flame thrower, the Ludlow Home Guard, at least, having one

Part of a Home Guard training manual illustrating the manoeuvring of a Smith Gun with the aid of toggle ropes. One of the men is grasping one of the narrow wheels which also provided a degree of overhead cover. The barrel of the gun is to the left. The limber which carried extra ammunition is not illustrated

specimen. The weapon was issued with nitrogen bottles on a scale decided by General HQ Home Forces, the nitrogen presumably projecting the burning mixture towards its target. 'Special corks, ten for each flamethrower' were required, as well as paraffin, matches and cotton waste. It is believed that it was usually moved about on a small trolley. One assumes that the job of operator wasn't very popular amongst the Home Guard![23]

More commonly found was the medieval-sounding flame fougasse. A South Shropshire Defence Plan mentions their use, as does a defence plan for Little Stretton (see illustration on p.46). A defence plan for Ludlow, prepared by the Home Guard Training School at Onibury in September 1943, indicates the sites of at least four locations for flame fougasses: on Temeside (where there was to be a minefield); two at Ludford and one by the approach to Dinham Bridge from the west. It is likely that there were others at different locations given the cheapness and potency of the weapon.[24] In October 1941 a memo from Park Hall Camp stated that the weapon consisted of a 40 gallon barrel with a special oil mixture which was to be buried in roadside banks. A small explosive charge was to be placed in a drainpipe situated behind the barrel on the giving of the code word 'Action Stations'. The ignition of the charge projected a stream of burning oil, two yards wide, a distance of at least 25 yards, the conflagration lasting about three minutes. They were normally to be employed in groups of four and emplaced on the advice of the Army's Sub Area Commander. Like other, heavier, weapons of the Home Guard they were to be used in prepared ambush positions, for example in cuttings, or ahead of an anti-tank block. The team for the weapon consisted of an observer and firer located a minimum of 25 yards from the obstacle, the

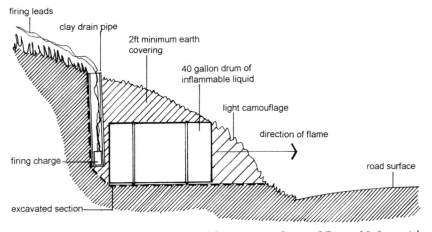

When fired the flame fougasse would project a sheet of flame 10 feet wide and 30 feet long, sufficient to disable a tank and its crew

firer having the leads and battery to fire the barrels. The team were enjoined to give serious consideration as to 'how to get away' once the weapon was fired![25]

The 2pdr anti-tank gun

This was a more conventional anti-tank weapon, passed on to the Home Guard following the issue to the Army of the more advanced 6pdr anti-tank gun. The weapon started to enter Home Guard service in late 1943. The use of the gun is noted in the *Fighting Book of Ist Battalion Salop Home Guard* prepared in September 1944. The 12 guns possessed by the Shrewsbury Battalion were in the charge of the No.2 HQ Platoon. Eleven weapons were to be emplaced on 'Action Stations' at strategic points around the town (for example, gun ten was to be in the Abbey churchyard, presumably firing towards The Column, with gun eleven to be by the castle on the north-west end of the station at the top of the ramp from Chester Street). Gun number 12 was to be held in reserve. In April 1944, 2pdr courses were run at the Western Command range at Altcar in Lancashire. By the time of its introduction into the Home Guard it would have had no chance of defeating the now heavier German tanks but would have been useful against lighter armoured vehicles. Anti-personnel ammunition was also available for the gun.[26]

Boys .55 anti-tank rifle

This was another weapon in the Shropshire Home Guard's armoury that was acquired via the Army; the 1st Battalion still possessed 30 in July 1944. Like the 2pdr anti-tank gun it would have proved of no value in defeating German tanks.

Firing Ranges

To use the weapons effectively required practice ranges but it seems that even in a rural county like Shropshire finding them was not always easy. Even in August 1944, the 2nd Battalion was still trying to find a Spigot Mortar range. The Home Guard was more successful in finding ranges for lighter weapons, the same battalion, for example, having ranges at: Llanymynych (rifle, Lewis machine gun, Sten, and Browning automatic rifle); Wood Lane, Llansilin, Harmer Hill, Cliffe and Sandford (rifle, Sten, grenades except phosphorous grenades); Rhosfach and Dolgoch (rifle, Sten, and Lewis machine gun and grenades. Grenades with phosphorous were only to be used if adequate steps had been taken to protect cattle); Berwick Park, Oswestry Coppice and Park Hall Camp (rifle, Sten, Browning automatic rifle and Lewis machine gun).

Chapter 4

Equipment and Communications for the Shropshire Home Guard

The unexpectedly massive response to the call for volunteers for the LDV led to the problem of not only arming but equipping the new force. On 29 May 1940 the Commander of the 2nd Battalion was able to write from Walford Manor to report that 'LDV armlets were being manufactured, denims were on order and FS [Field Service] caps were in stock.'[1]

The LDV armbands were soon replaced by Home Guard armbands: it was hoped that these, often temporarily worn with civilian clothing before the arrival of denims, would stop the invader shooting their wearers out of hand as terrorists. The surplus Army denim two piece working overalls were in the same cut as the serge uniform and were effectively overalls designed as work dress to be worn over the woollen khaki uniform. They were, however, shapeless and generally unpopular but at least they gave to the Home Guard a military look. When sufficient supplies of the standard woollen khaki uniform became available after the losses of stores at Dunkirk had been made up these were issued to the Home Guard, making their appearance almost identical to the Regular Army. A problem arose with men, usually officers, who had retained their First World War uniforms, still showing badges of a higher rank than those they held in the Home Guard. The issue of the new serge battle dress uniforms in place of the sloppy denim overalls alleviated this problem somewhat, but it was eventually agreed that officers might retain and use their old uniforms, as long as these were appropriately badged for Home Guard use![2]

When fully kitted-out the main differences in appearance between the Home Guard and their Regular Army colleagues, apart from weaponry, was that the former did not receive army webbing items, apart from the gas respirator bag and the revolver holster for officers. Special rubberised cotton khaki haversacks had to be manufactured as well as ammunition and grenade pouches, which took time to enter service. Leather gaiters were worn (these were darkened from their original tan colour to a less obtrusive dark brown or black using boot polish) and a leather belt was also worn. Before sufficient greatcoats were available a serge cape was issued which proved unpopular.[3] The issue of correctly sized greatcoats seems to have been a problem as one officer had to request, 'if anyone could produce a number 8 instead of a number 5 greatcoat the No.6 Company Commander would stand less chance of getting pneumonia'![4]

When the uniforms were first issued these aroused great interest, and their appearance was sometimes accompanied by remarks to their wearers such as 'you do look funny in it!' To add insult to injury, a spectator is also said to have told a harmless-looking 11th Battalion Home Guard member, 'you want to leave that rifle behind – you won't be so dangerous then'![5]

On 25 October 1940, the commander of the Shropshire Zone wrote to all units that 18 sizes of serge battledress were to be issued 'possibly shortly', and 'in order to avoid the trouble caused by the denims' it was 'absolutely necessary that approximately the correct sizes are given for the serge.' It is possible that the new uniform caused some members of the Home Guard to wear it too often, as an instruction had to be issued that 'wearing the uniform when not on duty or proceeding to or from duty' was to cease forthwith. Gradually the serge uniforms began to replace the denim ones, so that in October 1940 Zone HQ at Claremont Buildings, Shrewsbury was able to write to the 2nd Battalion that no more of the earlier uniforms were to be issued. There were 18 sizes of serge as against 12 of denim, and therefore there was no exact correspondence between them.[6] Many of the younger men took their uniform with them into the Army when called up, this consisting of the battledress (not denims or leather anklets), boots, field service cap less its badge, field dressing, greatcoat (not the Home Guard serge cape), knitted gloves, anti-gas-ointment, eye shields and the gas respirator.[7]

Standard issue Army boots were supplied and it was felt that these should not require repairs for at least one year. Commanders were enjoined to check that if there was any indication that the boots were being used for purposes other than for Home Guard use, then the volunteer would have to pay for the repair.[8] Given that many of the men were not young, the requirement for special footwear was broached in Army Council Instruction 1070 of June 1941. For those enrolled before 1 June 1941 a cash allowance of 22s. 6d. (£1 12½p) in lieu of the issue boots would be granted, provided:

a) a medical certificate was supplied confirming that issue boots could not be worn.

b) a certificate from the man's commanding officer, countersigned by the Secretary of the relevant Territorial Army Association, was forthcoming stating that standard issue boots had not been issued, and

c) there was proof of purchase of the special boots.

On or after 1 June 1941, however, no man was to be accepted into the Home Guard who was unable to wear issue boots unless he was willing to purchase his own pair.[9]

At the standing down of the organisation in late 1944 the following items could be retained: caps, anklets, battle dress, boots and 'capes anti-gas' (capes together with an anti-gas respirator formed part of the Regular Army's anti-gas equipment).[10] If, on leaving the Home Guard prior to stand down, a volunteer wished to purchase his boots the cost was still 22s. 6d.

but less 1 shilling per month whilst the boots had been in the possession of the Home Guard member.[11]

The clothing issue to the Home Guard was quite basic, especially given that many of its early members were elderly. To offer a little extra help the Women's Voluntary Service from their headquarters in Shrewsbury wrote to Captain Jebb of the 2nd Battalion (Ellesmere) in July 1940 that 'Our working parties will be in a position to supply necessary comforts e.g. scarves, socks, helmets [presumably balaclavas], mittens and gloves. Please send us a list of your requirements as soon as possible.'[12]

The woollen battledress blouse of a captain in the 4th Battalion of the Shropshire Home Guard. The HOME GUARD and SHR 4 badges can be clearly seen. This uniform is on display in the Shropshire Regimental Museum

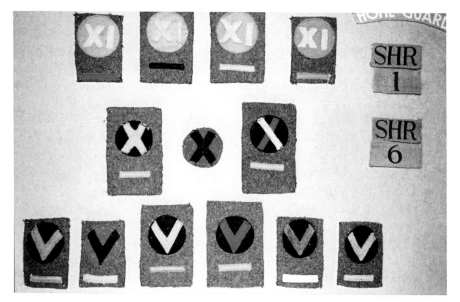

The Wellington Group battalions (5th, 10th and 11th Shropshire Home Guard) did not wear the standard Home Guard battalion badge. For reasons that are unclear they wore a unique type of badge using coloured felt patches and Roman numerals. The numeral indicated the battalion and the backing and bars in different colours is believed to have represented companies and platoons within the battalions

Signalling and Communications

It was necessary that some form of communications system be established for the new force as quickly as possible. The Shropshire Home Guard was initially reliant on runners, carrier pigeons, despatch riders and the civilian telephone system, although this latter was very vulnerable to sabotage attack. Hence telephone exchanges were regarded as vulnerable points (VPs) and the General Post Office, which also ran the country's telephone network, established its own Home Guard Battalions. Somewhat later, the Home Guard was encouraged to use the communications facilities at nearby searchlight sites and later still eventually portable army-issue radio telegraphy/ wireless telegraphy (R/T, W/T) sets were introduced. The carrier pigeon still had a part to play. For example A Company of the 7th Battalion could boast a flight time of only six minutes from the pigeon loft in Church Stretton to the battalion HQ in Craven Arms, a distance of seven miles. In 1940 the Government had ordered the destruction of all homing pigeons for fear of their use by fifth columnists, except those used by the Home Guard and other military formations.[13]

The need for the Home Guard to take on additional duties such as signalling was resisted by some commanders. For example Colonel Morris Eyton wrote in July 1941 to the Army's Oswestry Sub Area that to take on these additional responsibilities was 'impossible' in the men's few available free hours, and a suggestion was made by him that a refresher course be arranged for old signallers. He went on to make the point that there was 'some danger of over-regimentation of the Home Guard and the breaking-up of the movement altogether, particularly in agricultural areas where very long hours were being worked and where everyone knows how these compare with those in a [Army] camp. My duty as Battalion CO is to point out and hope that the matter will not be pressed'.[14]

In October 1941 Army Council Instruction 2045 dealt with the Home Guard signalling organisation, specifying that each Zone or General Headquarters (GHQ) authority was to employ a motorcycle despatch rider using his own motorcycle, up to two per battalion being used within each Zone or group. Two months later ACI 2502 stated that Army issue crash helmets plus protective clothing were to be provided. In November 1942 a Western Command Instruction stated that Army WT sets numbers 18, 21 and 38 were to be issued shortly to the Home Guard.[15]

That these were issued to Colonel Morris Eyton's battalion, despite his earlier reservations, is indicated by a memo he issued to A Company of the 2nd Battalion at the beginning of September 1944 entitled 'HG RT code SECRET' regarding the issue of a new vocabulary to be used with the Home Guard R/T code. It noted that this was to be 'always kept under lock and key' due to the regular necessity of rearranging the vocabulary. A 'Unit card No.1' was enclosed to replace the existing one. The new cards were 'only to be completed in pencil so these could be used again if there was further alteration'. The card was divided into a number of lettered and numbered squares, the sequence of which must have been varied from time to time. For example, square '08' might indicate 'attack' whilst 'x' might indicate 'send'. The recipient would have the same card and could pick up the message.[16]

In 1940 a number of codewords had been introduced to be used in communications in the event of threatened or actual invasion. The codewords varied over time but their intent was to generate three levels of preparedness, the first a general state of readiness, the second that invasion was believed to be imminent and that landings by parachutists are likely, and the third that the invasion has occurred or that the enemy was believed to be in range of the unit. On the issue of this last alert each company's posts, including permanent roadblocks and guard posts around vulnerable points, were to be continually manned, bringing with them rations for 24 hours and their anti-gas equipment. At the roadblocks everything would have been checked to ensure that the hairpin blocks could have been quickly put in place. Mobile sections were to be ready, whilst all motor vehicles and petrol installations likely to fall into enemy hands were to be immobilised. Despatch riders were to station themselves at the battalion HQ. Catering committees were to prepare for feeding the Home Guard after the first 24 hours. Carrier pigeons were to be made ready, and medical facilities were to be prepared.

In the late summer of 1940 the following series of codewords had been introduced:

WOLF – genuine landings were to be expected.

YPRES – maintenance of an existing state of alert, with the manning of important defence positions.

CROMWELL – imminent invasion by paratroopers was expected.

OLIVER – invasion has occurred and the enemy was within range. There was to be day and night manning of all posts.

However, this first set of codewords caused confusion. There was the pronunciation and spelling of Ypres, for example, and the conjunction of Cromwell and Oliver could create confusion. The interpretation of what each word stood for also produced confusion, different Commands having different interpretations as witnessed in Western Command in September 1940 when in a practice exercise in Eastern Command 'Cromwell' was mentioned. This was copied to other Commands, who took it to mean that the enemy was expected in their vicinity. And so a revised set of codewords was issued:

ARRAS – extreme tension: parachutist attacks, the sabotaging of industrial production and output was to be expected.

NEWTON – conditions were considered to be very favourable for invasion, with airborne landings very likely. The Home Guard, however, was not to be mustered due the loss of manpower that would result in industry and agriculture.

ACTION STATIONS – invasion imminent.

OLIVER – invasion has occurred.

The *Fighting Book of 1st Battalion Salop Home Guard*, prepared in September 1944 records a further set of codewords then in use:

NORMAL – state of readiness existing when invasion considered likely in immediate future and raids possible. Troops to be at eight hours readinesss.

BILL – enemy may interfere with invasion (D-Day) by sabotage. 'Unless Ireland is invaded it is unlikely that the Welsh Border Sub Division will bear the first brunt of an enemy attack.' (A scheme codenamed 'Bill' had been prepared to protect the road and rail routes through Shrewsbury against possible enemy sabotage attacks during the D-Day period.)

STAND TO – situation favourable for invasion.

ACTION STATIONS – immediate threat of invasion.

OLIVER – executive order to muster.

LIDDELL – attack on Shrewsbury expected or imminent. (Lt Col Liddell was the commanding officer of the battalion at that time).

BOUNCER – 'Bugbear' may be used shortly.

BUGBEAR – raids by airborne troops expected.

BUGBEAR STAND DOWN – revert to 'Normal'.[17]

The position concerning communications was summarised late in the war in a memorandum written by an unnamed Lieutenant Colonel in the Home Guard and distributed to UK Home Guard units. His comments would have applied across the Shropshire Home Guard. He noted firstly that the communications problem was the most slippery of all as there did not seem to be anything laid down officially and the provision of signals equipment was so scanty. He pointed out that the organisation had a number of commitments including the protection of vulnerable points, the manning of strongpoints and roadblocks, patrolling, and a counter-attack role. As a result he said it was necessary to site HQs to allow for easy communications with each other, that

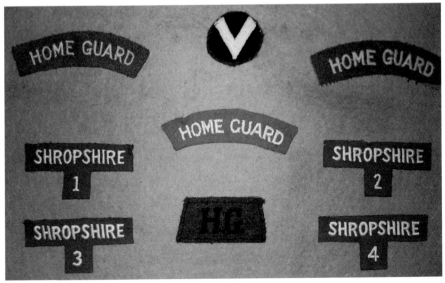

*Badges of the post-war Home Guard on display
in the Shropshire Regimental Museum*

maintenance of the Post Office telephone system was most important, and that commanders must have and keep handy up to date lists of local telephone exchanges and relevant telephone numbers.

He then went on to pose a number of questions and suggestions. Despatch riders were of real value in making special runs – but were they always positioned at the right locations? Motorcycles had to be kept properly maintained to be effective, but commanders should consider using 'push bikes', too. He noted that wireless sets, though of short range, were invaluable if carefully distributed and the operatives well trained – and there was an adequate battery supply. He advised the preparation of a signals plan that fitted in with other bodies such as the General Post Office, the Observer Corps, local airfields, and the Civil Defence force. In the Oswestry area, for example, the Home Guard was encouraged to use the local searchlight units' communications facilities in an emergency.[18]

Chapter 5

Training the Shropshire Home Guard

It was all very well creating the new force but it had to be trained as well as armed: the former would prove to be as an enormous a task as the latter. Only half of the Craven Arms volunteers, for example, had had past military experience.[1] Initially the 'old sweats' of 1914-18 had come forward 'to have another bash at the Boche', but with conscription, introduced in 1942, the problem of training became even greater as the complexities and responsibilities of the organisation had also increased.

After preliminary instruction in the care and use of arms, the real problem was in securing enough instructors for the more advanced training. In Shropshire the answer lay with the Infantry Training Corps of the KSLI which offered training courses from the start (the Shropshire Home Guard would eventually be affiliated to the regiment). The training corps soon 'proved splendid in its co-operation, providing examples, for instance, of good and bad defence tactics'.[2]

Structured training also began to be offered for Shropshire and adjacent counties as early as June 1940 by Lt Col Otter-Barry's Training School at Draycott near Claverley. Amongst other training courses that sprang up in 1940 as a result of private initiatives, the best known was that at Osterley Park near London. This was run by Tom Wintringham and others who had had some military experience not just in the First World War but in fighting during the Spanish Civil War. Wintringham wrote wartime articles for the periodical *Picture Post* together with a number of books including *New Ways of Warfare*. He was very critical of the 'spit and polish' type of training beloved of the Army and many Home Guard commanders: this, coupled with his communist politics, doomed Osterley Park to a brief life and it was closed by the War Office. He did, subsequently, spend time lecturing to the Home Guard on what he saw as the new ways of warfare, including to the Wellington Battalion, and he probably influenced the setting up of the three

An early photograph of the officers of the No.3 GHQ Home Guard Training School at Stokesay Court. (Courtesy of Caroline Magnus)

General Headquarters (GHQ) training centres, one being at Stokesay Court in Shropshire. Whether any members of the LDV went to Osterley is not known, but many will have attended the courses at Draycott.[3]

This latter opened, equipped with a borrowed British Legion tent, at the sand quarry in the village. Gradually the school grew and a *Musketry Manual* (this archaic term remained in use in army circles) was published by Otter-Barry. The school's initial aim was to train instructors but the numbers attending plus the pressures of anti-invasion needs in 1940 meant that instruction was also provided directly to LDV members. By 1941 the whole of the Salop Zone was using the school together with the South Staffs Zone. The school was the only one of its type in the West Midlands at this time, and from June to October ten hours of training was being provided on each Sunday, mainly in the use of the rifle. Early in 1941 the Army's North Wales District gave permission for the appointment of three Permanent Staff Instructors (PSI), and two huts were erected on the site. About this time, also, the TA gave the school a grant of £20 per month; by this time between 80 and 100 students were attending each Sunday plus a lesser number on the weekday evening courses. From early 1941 the school issued certificates to supervisors for various types of grenade throwing, with later certificates representing the same standard as the Western Command Weapon Training School at Altcar in Lancashire for the Spigot Mortar, grenades, Sten, rifle, machine guns etc. From June 1942 the school's policy altered:

at the suggestion of Major-General Lord Bridgeman (Director-General of the Home Guard from 1941-44) the school now confined itself to weapons training, and to turning out officers and NCOs as unit instructors. Courses now became more limited but of a longer duration. The school by this time had acquired a lecture hall, a canteen, a store, an ammunition magazine, and an office. There were ranges for various types of weapons with classes now on both Saturdays and Sundays with optional accommodation one and half miles away. Since its inception, applications had always exceeded its capacity.[4]

As the war progressed Permanent Staff Instructors began to be attached to battalions: such a recruit was found in a J.H. Evans of the Royal Welch Fusiliers in November 1941 for the 2nd Battalion of the Shropshire Home Guard. By the time that the Shropshire Home Guard was due to be stood down the 7th Battalion had three PSIs attached to its ranks.

The complexities of modern warfare plus the fact that there was little in the way of weapons training manuals for the Home Guard, led to a proliferation of privately published books and pamphlets by military publishers such as Gale and Polden, and Bernards. Not all were of equal value and the War Office endeavoured to recommend those that were, although it is unclear if such could be purchased out of Home Guard training funds. Some bordered on the fatuous such as one entitled *Unarmed Combat. Your Answer to Invasion- Ju Jitsu*. The publications of the military publishers Gale and Polden received general official approval, for example one entitled *The Fighting Patrol* by Colonel Wade, though this was apparently not to be purchased out of 'funds'. Official training instructions started during the brief life of the LDV: for example Instruction No.3 dealt with German parachutists. These were then followed by a regular issue of Home Guard Instructions and Information Circulars.[5] In addition, the War Office produced a series of instructional films on such subjects as anti-vehicle obstacles and German airborne troops.

To conduct exercises across open country the Home Guard had powers to take over and use land for training purposes. Instructions were given in Army Council Instruction 1069 of 26 June 1941 on how to proceed: there had to be prior arrangement with the landowner, and (of course!) the arrangement was to be without charge to the public purse. The Home Guard had powers under the Defence Regulation 52 to seek an order from a Regular Army officer in order to take over land for training purposes. Any claims for damages were to be sent to the Claims Commission.[6]

In addition to formal training, battalions drew up 'schemes' with their parent Army unit for realistic exercises usually involving imaginary airborne or seaborne landings. One such was the exercise held at Clun in the 7th Battalion's area on Sunday 20 July 1941, which has been mentioned in chapter 2. The scheme was that enemy forces had landed on the Welsh coast and had reached a line running from Bishops Castle through Clun to Knighton. The Home Guard were to concentrate on defending nodal points, concentrating on all round defence, holding out until relieved by Regulars. The 'defenders' were D Company (Clun) whose perimeter ran in a half mile radius of the town. It was ordered that roadblocks were not to be erected. The 'enemy' was E Company (Bishops Castle) and I Company (Bucknell), plus elements from the army's Vehicle Maintenance School at The Grove at Craven Arms. Their role was to reconnoitre and attempt the capture of the town, but all standing crops were out of bounds.

Following the 'battle' a summary stated that no gaps had been found in the defences but that D Company's reserve platoon was wasted as it received no information on what was happening. The defenders were criticised for taking no decisive action, awaiting the enemy's initiative. Despite this the umpires felt that 'The men all worked extremely well but the lack of leadership is serious'. The absence of blank ammunition was also considered 'serious' (presumably it would have added realism). Another point was that fifth column impersonations were 'being overdone' but that cars had been left unlocked and unattended and these could be used by a potential enemy.

As for the attacking force, their attempts to co-ordinate attacks were unsuccessful, chiefly due to the nature of the ground. Attacks came in from all directions in over 50 minutes – 'more than the Germans could do'.

As for the platoon attacks, these were well carried out, taking full advantage of the covered lines of approach, but platoon commanders had underestimated the difficulties in effective communications in such close country. Armoured vehicles must have been employed in the exercise as their attack was put in with 'dash and determination'. Further suggestions were made that in future use be made of a 'token' road block barrier. Street fighting was considered badly done, the men advancing 'like a crowd leaving a football match'. It was felt that if a Lewis gun had opened up there would have been 75% casualties.

Yet more observations noted that fields of fire were poor but this was mainly due to the nature of the ground. There was an absence of any natural positions for the Lewis guns but their use in a mobile role was felt to be 'excellent' and to be considered for the future. The Norman castle must have been brought into the plan as the men in the castle post had made the error of exposing themselves on the skyline. Cover generally was criticised, as the men went for obvious positions such as woods that an enemy would bombard, especially as the locality had many dominating points. Inter communications were considered well thought out, but not enough use was made of this facility; unfortunately we are not told how these operated.

A later exercise was that at Rednal on 31 July 1941 when it was observed that: 'In thirty hours the Home Guard has been transformed from an all too voluntary body into a well-disciplined force'. A facetious comment was made: 'There was an immense outcry for beer on Saturday night – if it had proved possible to supply this, many Home Guard would have been able to concentrate more fully on the affairs in hand.' However, 'No account was taken of age and the hardening process was violent.' It was recommended that the men were not asked to manoeuvre over wide areas. Instead, vulnerable points for defending should be selected or transport supplied. Additional training was felt to be required in bayonet fighting, gas drill, bomb throwing and anti-aircraft defence. Possibly this exercise was connected with the new airfield being built at Rednal that opened in April 1942.[7]

The success of the German parachute and glider-borne troops in 1940 had left an exaggerated but indelible impression on the British High Command. How vulnerable such troops could be was demonstrated in the battle for Crete in May 1941 when some 1,600 German paratroopers lost their lives. Subsequent exercises in Shropshire were, perhaps, representative of many others held around the country. That held on 19 August 1941 by the Home Guard in Ellesmere had the objectives of testing decision making; practising getting the men into position; and testing abilities in scouting.

For the purposes of the exercise it was deemed that the local Home Guard commanding officer had received information from the Army's Officer Commanding Troops (Ellesmere District) that the hall porter at Ellesmere College had reported 60 young men with heavy suitcases arriving by private bus shortly after 7pm. They had said that they were attending a summer school there. The porter's suspicions were aroused as the school was not due to open until the following day. The men demanded access to the dormitories. The local Home Guard intended to keep the school under observation and to surround it with concealed picquets to prevent anyone entering or leaving. The mobile reserve was to be kept ready. Additionally at 19.25 hours a local woman had reported seeing lot of white parachutes carrying packages: these were to be kept under observation.[8]

Another exercise involved the 'enemy' using seaplanes to disgorge troops on the Mere, a form of attack the Germans had used in the capture of Rotterdam in 1940. What isn't mentioned in the scenario is that, like other large stretches of water, the Mere had been obstructed by a floating barrier during the war against such an eventuality.

A further tactical exercise was held in the same area on 26 August 1941. The objectives this time were to test: the knowledge of the ground in a vital area; the arrangements for the defence of the Company HQ; and the dispositions of the machine gun troop to command the Mere. On this occasion the background was that the 'Officer Commanding Garrison' had received from the 'Officer Commanding Troops (Ellesmere District) the following report:

> Helped by low cloud the enemy have landed 40 to 50 troops from seaplanes now floating on the Mere. One party is moving through the grounds of Ellesmere House towards the Bowling Green. Others are moving towards the old sand hole having crossed Sandy Lane. More planes are heard overhead and are expected to come down on the Mere with reinforcements.
>
> The Home Guard are to deny them the [commanding position of the] bowling green, to protect HQ [the Drill Hall] and to destroy the reinforcements landing on the Mere and to take up positions accordingly.

In the operation the Home Guard were allowed to enter private gardens but were to avoid damaging them.[9]

Another exercise again involved a threat from airborne troops and was held on 2 September 1941. This time the objectives were to practice the training of unit leaders in mutual support; to train all ranks in the use of ground and cover; and to train the machine gun troop in the choice of suitable positions. This time the scenario proposed was as follows: 'Enemy airborne troops have landed west of the canal north of Ouston and have been destroyed except for six that have taken cover north-east of Newnes. Further landings on Ouston may be attempted. The Home Guard are to take the Newnes party alive, and any further landings are to be promptly dealt with. The Ouston ground is to be commanded by machine gun fire.'[10]

Bryan Powell's father, Albert Edward, worked for Sankeys at Ketley, which during the war produced Spitfire components, and was in their Home Guard unit, part of the 5th Battalion (Wellington). Bryan recollects the story his father told him of an exercise in Long Lane near the RAF's Bratton airfield. The object was for the local Home Guard to test the airfield's defences and to 'capture' it. They had to crawl one and a half miles from their start point at Wappenshall which was south-east of the airfield. Having completed this laborious approach, apparently undetected, they found the site devoid of RAF personnel apart from one airman in a hut who said that he had drawn the short straw and been told to 'hang on until the Home Guard arrived.' The rest of his comrades had decided to go to the nearby pub![11]

Lockley Percy Evans never went outside the county on Home Guard courses but recollects two weekends spent on duty at Church Stretton Railway Station (in which town he also fell asleep whilst on guard at the back of the Territorial Army hut), and also time spent on the Long Mynd, perhaps on anti-parachutist exercises. At church parades he would see the horses of the local mounted Home Guard that belonging to the better off local farmers and their sons. Despite this distinction he felt that they all mixed well. (A number of Home Guard mounted patrols had been authorised in 1940 for the patrolling of sparsely populated areas of countryside. An allowance of 12 shillings (60p) per month was given. In May 1942 new patrols were authorised including ones in the 7th Battalion area where an increase to 15 shillings (75p) per month was made for the maintenance of each horse and its equipment. Members of each patrol were allowed to wear riding breeches with puttees and the peaked service dress cap.)

Weekend Home Guard exercises were carried out on the Long Mynd and at Wall under Heywood where his platoon had to take prisoner a neighbouring unit. He remembers 'climbing all over the hills, making a racket with thunder flashes' – and then retiring to the 'pub at Wall'. From there he walked back to Cardington.

In addition to occasional church parades he had to be present every Sunday for exercises. There was the firing of live ammunition and throwing of live

grenades on The Lawley where the public had to be stopped from using nearby footpaths. Apart from the rifle the only other weapon he used was the Sten submachine gun, which he didn't enjoy using. Other exercises involved running whilst wearing the service gas respirator which he described as very difficult.[12]

An interesting account showing the timetable of an exercise is contained in the 2nd Battalion A Company Orders dated 1 October 1941. In this case assistance would be provided by officers and

Men of the No.2 Platoon of A Company Home Guard Mounted Unit of the 7th Battalion wearing the peaked service cap with the badge of the parent regiment, the KSLI, on its front. (Shropshire Archives)

Certificate of Proficiency
HOME GUARD

On arrival at the Training Establishment, Primary Training Centre or Recruit Training Centre, the holder must produce this Certificate at once for the officer commanding, together with Certificate A if gained in the Junior Training Corps or Army Cadet Force.

PART I. I hereby certify that (Rank) Private (Name and initials) EVANS L.P.

of "A" ~~Battery~~ Company 7th Shropshire ~~Regiment~~ Battalion HOME GUARD has qualified in the Proficiency Badge tests as laid down in the pamphlet "Qualifications for, and Conditions governing the Award of the Home Guard Proficiency Badges and Certificates" for the following subjects :—

Subject	Date	Initials
1. General knowledge (all candidates)	16.12.43.	
2. Rifle	16.12.43.	SGO
3. 36 M Grenade	16.12.43.	
*4. (a) Other weapon Sten Carbine	16.1.44	
(b) ~~Signalling~~		
*5. (a) Battlecraft, (b) ~~Coast Artillery, (c) Heavy A.A. Bty.~~ ~~work, (d) "Z" A.A. Battery work, (e) Bomb Disposal,~~ ~~(f) Watermanship, (g) M.T.~~	16.1.44.	
*6. (a) Map Reading, (b) ~~Field works, (c)~~ First Aid ⟨MR⟩	16.1.44.	

Date 16 JAN 1944 194...   Signature H C Meredith major
President or Member of the Board.

Date...............194....   Signature............................
President or Member of the Board.

Date...............194....   Signature............................
President or Member of the Board.

Date...............194....   Signature............................
President or Member of the Board.

Date...............194....   Signature............................
President or Member of the Board.

PART II. I certify that (Rank) PTE. (Name and initials) EVANS. L.P.

of A. ~~Battery~~ Company ~~Regiment~~ Battalion HOME GUARD, having duly passed the Proficiency tests in the subjects detailed above in accordance with the pamphlet and is hereby authorized to wear the Proficiency Badge as laid down in Regulations for the Home Guard, Vol. 1, 1942, para. 41d.

Date 16.1. 1944   Signature A⟨...⟩ordon Lt col

Commanding NO. 7 BATTALION, H.G.
SHROPSHIRE HOME GUARDS

PART III. If the holder joins H.M. Forces, his Company or equivalent Commander will record below any particulars which he considers useful in assessing the man's value on arrival at the T.E., P.T.C., R.T.C., e.g. service, rank, duties on which employed, power of leadership, etc.

Date...............194....   Signature............................
O.C.

* Delete where not applicable.

The Certificate of Service issued to Lockley Percy Evans after his service in the Home Guard

NCOs from the locally-based 236 Searchlight Regiment Royal Artillery (presumably they also provided the umpires):

> 10.30 Muster at The Boathouse Restaurant. Each man to be in battledress with haversack, greatcoat or cape, 'tin hat' [steel helmet], and gas respirator.
> 11.00 Arms inspection to include rifles, shotguns, Lewis with spare part boxes, magazine carriers (to contain no live rounds), Browning machine guns and Northover Projectors.
> 11.45 Oteley Park field training.
> 13.30 Dinner at The Boathouse.
> 15.00 Lecture on reconnaissance.
> 15.30 Reconnaissance exercise on Castle Field.
> 17.30 Tea at The Boathouse.
> 18.30 Night exercise.
> 18.30 Criticism by umpires.

Each man was to have haversack rations for the day (dinner and tea was presumably eaten in The Boathouse Restaurant) and could claim 3 shillings (15p) subsistence. Farm workers with milking duties had permission for absence between the times of dinner and teatime.[13]

In January 1942 a memo from Shropshire Zone HQ regarding away courses noted that only 259 out of a total of 600 Home Guard officers had attended those courses of 6 to 7 days duration. It went on to say that the 'outstanding value of the Claverley and Copthorne [Barracks] courses cannot be overstated' and 'officers face at times problems keeping up the interests of their men, who have to assemble after long days of work, *many still without rifles* [author's italics]'. Officers were to make every effort to take advantage of senior level courses at Peover (Cheshire), Stokesay (formerly at Ludlow), and Denbies (Surrey).[14]

A training programme for the 4th Battalion, which covered the Bayston Hill, Condover and Minsterley area, and probably dating from the middle of the war included a weekly talk or exercise for each of the 28 platoons covering one of the following: map reading, the Sten gun, the Lewis light machine gun, the machine gun (presumably Browning), wireless communications, 'firing positions', the duties of the sentry, field craft, battle craft, the rifle-reconnaissance patrols. In addition there were exercises on Sundays covering platoon attack, battle craft, patrolling, camouflage, map reading, range practice at Westbury, the 'standing patrol' and anti-parachutist patrolling.[15]

Whilst there seemed to be a great emphasis on training in the 2nd Battalion, not all was well, however. On 2 February 1942, Colonel Morris Eyton wrote from Walcot Manor to the commanding officer of No.1 Company (on 1 March 1942 companies changed from being identified by numbers to a letter system; on that date No.1 Company became A Company) at the Drill Hall, Ellesmere as follows:

> I cannot help but feel disappointed at the inability of your Company to fall in with training arrangements directed from Queens Head [the Batallion HQ]. Yours is the only Company to do so. The object of the plan is to get the machinery into being for a far more careful record of attendances, necessary in future, and also to ensure training is systematic and progressive.
>
> I have no intention of interfering with company arrangements but the Sub Area [Army] and Zone are continually asking to be informed about what is going on and unless some pre-arranged programme can be submitted, unnecessary telephoning and correspondence is inevitable. I would be grateful if you would reconsider.

Added to the memo, presumably by the recipient is the comment: 'Progressive beyond ... [illegible] next week is eyewash.'[16]

An innovation spreading from the Commandos and other special forces was unarmed combat. The principal proponents were Captains Fairbairn and Sykes, late of the Shanghai police, who had written books on the subject for Home Guard consumption. Perhaps as a result, in February 1942, Shropshire Zone wrote to all Home Guard battalions that a Sergeant Ross was 'almost entirely available to the Home Guard for unarmed combat training.[17]

More formal courses were also established at Dodington Hall, just over the border in Cheshire, announced in Western Command Instruction No.1256 of July 1942. These trained senior officers in the choice and organisation of defensive positions in both rural and urban situations. Some exercises may have been becoming too realistic for the public, as an instruction went out in the middle of the war ordering that any exercises involving the wearing of real or replica German uniforms were to be referred to HQ first.[18]

From the summer of 1942, after the introduction of Home Guard conscription, Civil Defence training was introduced to add to the list of other skills its members were expected to acquire. All were expected to have a knowledge of the Civil Defence organisation, and those members forming parts of Rescue Parties or part of Decontamination Squads were to undergo six hours of practical training, and those also carrying out Air Raid Warden duties were to attend a four hour course.

Other, later, exercises recorded in Shropshire are 'Salop', 'Orange', 'Banana' and 'Salsig', the latter held on 20 January 1943 to test communications between the Home Guard, RAF and other bodies. 'Queen' was held on 21 February 1943 and included a descent by the Parachute Regiment where the sound of light artillery was to be replicated by a 'short shake of pebbles in a tin', and the firing of a Northover Projector by the discharge of a thunder flash. Exercise 'Nodal' was held on 2 May 1943 where 'a German landing had occurred in Tremadoc' and the Home Guard were to practice the manning of nodal defences. The following month another signals exercise was held under the name of 'Castle'.[19]

Realistic and detailed indoor 'battle' exercises were also conducted using sand trays or large cloth models of the company's or battalion's locality.(what we would now call war games). Such a one was that held at the Drill Hall in Ironbridge in July 1943. The 'enemy' was to consist of the Commanding Officer, the Adjutant and four officers of the 5th Battalion. 'Own troops' were to be provided by Company HQs. In the given scenario the invasion of the country had started on 7 July, and an enemy attempt to relieve pressure on its main assault forces by trying to disorganise supplies and reinforcements by landing airborne forces in the Midlands with Wolverhampton and Birmingham was suspected. Troop carrying aircraft had been seen on French airfields on 10 July. Code word NEWTON had been issued. On 11 July occurred the bombing of Birmingham and Wolverhampton with raids on Shropshire airfields. Parachutists were now landing at Condover (there was an airfield here), Dorrington, Pontesbury and Church Stretton. The Code word OLIVER had been issued by the 6th Battalion. Condover airfield had been captured.

The Home Guard had been ordered to take up positions to defend crossing points for Situation 'B' (possibly an attack from the west). Enemy columns were on the move and the Condover Army Motor Transport park had been captured: the enemy was now assumed to be fully mobile. Enemy attacks on Cressage Bridge had occurred, the police at Much Wenlock reported an enemy column with machine guns and mortars, its strength 800 men, and they were proceeding towards Buildwas. The enemy had orders to 'attack and capture the crossings of the Severn from Buildwas to Jackfield. The enemy was taking up positions on the high ground to the north of the river one mile in depth.'

On the large model, black and white cards would represent the enemy, own troops would be represented by 'various cards'. 'Anti-tank roadblocks' would be represented by a red cross, but the 'blocks' would not be 'erected' unless ordered by HQ. The accompanying guidance for umpires noted that each Company locality had a draft Fighting Book: 'one object is to find faults and omissions in the Books vis-a-vis the supply of ammunition, the arrangements for the treating of casualties, 'fooding', and sanitary arrangements'.[20]

One exercise demonstrating the potential firepower of a Battalion mid-war was that of 'Chirk' held on 3 October 1943 by the 2nd Battalion to demonstrate the defences of a vulnerable point (Chirk Bridge). At Lower Chirk Bank there was a Northover Projector and three men as well as a Blacker Bombard with five men. On the canalside there was another Northover Projector with three men as well as a Browning heavy machine gun with three belts of ammunition. There was also a 'reinforced cottage' with a Lewis machine gun – the Home Guard were encouraged to make use of existing buildings where these were in a suitable position and fortify them with barbed wire and sandbags. On the bridge itself were four riflemen with hand grenades, whilst riflemen were positioned in the Old Post Office. On the aqueduct there were men armed with two Discharger Cups (EY rifles), one Lewis machine gun and grenades, and a similarly armed force was at 'Via West'. Riflemen with grenades were positioned in Penylan Wood, whilst at the railway was a Blacker Bombard with riflemen, and riflemen with a Lewis machine gun were also in Oaklands Wood.[21]

Two months later the same battalion held Exercise 'Rednal' where a German attack attempted to seize the airfield. The object of the exercise was to test how the Home Guard communicated with the airfield's Battle HQ.

Training could, however, be disrupted due to the demands of the country to produce as much food as possible (fortunately wartime summers appear to have been good although there were several extremely cold winters). For example, Exercise 'Rail' (to practice patrolling a railway line) planned for 19 July 1943 had to be postponed due to an early corn harvest and late hay harvest. Just under a year later Welsh Border Sub District at Rhadley House, Kingsland, Shrewsbury wrote on 19 May 1944 that due to the demands of milking, training was to be elastic. Additionally, a six day camp due to be held at the end of May was not to take place, apparently due to there being no compensation for loss of earnings.[22]

An idea of the attention to training (as well as the practical difficulties in wartime) is given in Home Guard Instruction No.48 of July 1942 which laid down that members might be called upon to perform training and operational duties for 48 hours in each period of 4 weeks, and where possible, 24 hours of the 48 was to be devoted to training. It admitted that many men 'cannot do more', so training was to be devoted to the actual job they had to do. The training could be divided into two sections: basic, for example the use of

Men of the 2nd Battalion at a camp in the grounds of Boreatton Park in 1943 or 1944. In comparison with the earlier photographs of the Hordley Home Guard on page 21 the men appear youthful. All wear their anti-gas respirators slung in the 'alert' position together with steel helmets some of which are covered by a camouflage net. (Shropshire Archives)

Another photograph of members of the 2nd Battalion at Boreatton. Of note are the three 'armoured cars': civilian saloons fitted with steel plate. This group are probably part of a mobile battle platoon as they seem heavily armed. The man third from the left is holding an EY/DC rifle. Near him is a Lewis gun on an anti-aircraft mounting with, in the centre of the photograph, a similar gun on a ground mounting. To the right is a Browning medium machine gun on a tripod with its ammunition box on the left-hand side of the gun. All the men wear blackened leather gaiters.
(Shropshire Archives)

weapons, field craft and minor tactics, street fighting, patrolling and tank-hunting, and then the application of these to the actual job they would have to carry out in their own locality. By this time more emphasis was being put on training instructors who could then 'train the rest':

> We have two Home Guard schools and are now opening a third [one of these was Stokesay Court]. These schools give five day courses in tactics and weapon training to battalion, company or platoon commanders. Many officers who cannot get away to attend have formed five travelling wings touring the Commands giving instruction. They are a great success and we hope to increase the number to twenty-seven but it is difficult to find the numbers of instructors required as we also have to find a large number of other officers for Home Guard schools and the travelling wings will absorb 186 instructors, and in addition we are aiming to give Home Guard units a whole time training officer for every three battalions in addition to the full time adjutant, QM, and permanent staff instructor in each battalion.
>
> In addition to the training at special schools vacancies are allotted to the Home Guard at Command Weapon Training Schools with special wings or we devote whole courses to the Home Guard. We are also starting schools for street fighting [one was in Birmingham]. We help instructors by issuing special Home Guard training films, plus training pamphlets. In addition, the Regular Army runs exercises for the Home Guard at weekends, or will bring them into their own exercises dealing with anti-invasion problems. These are a valuable form of training but it is not all plain sailing. In some areas we are able to affiliate every Home Guard unit with an Army unit and the result is excellent. Unfortunately the HG is most numerous in those areas where regular troops are fewest, so the full benefit cannot be achieved.
>
> Then again, the big exercises of the Army last many days and nights and cover wide areas. Opposing commanders do not know in advance exactly where the battle will be. It has been found that although the Home Guard is willing to turn out at night *after working all day at their normal jobs* [author's italics] it is impossible to ensure that they will become involved in the battle and it is disheartening for the Home Guard if they are called out and spend a cold and miserable night without anything happening. It is a real difficulty and the best we can do is to warn the Home Guard of the whole area of the exercise and that they may be required, Control Staff can call out, at the last moment, those in suitable localities *and willing to turn out* [author's italics]. Sometimes this works, sometimes not. I explain this as the Home Guard are apt to wonder why they do not take part in more

Regular Army exercises, though they would complain if they had to spend a sleepless, fruitless night to no useful purpose.

In spite of the difficulties in dealing with a part time force of men, most of whom are employed in other important work, the training of the Home Guard has made great progress.[23]

A document recording individual training and relating to one of the Bridgnorth companies of the 8th Battalion gives an interesting insight into the progress (or otherwise) of those being trained. Sergeant J. Gough, born in 1899 was issued with rifle number 409104 and attended a one-day gas course on 22 Feb 1942 and 'Blitz' and Sten courses in July 1942. He had trained on the Northover Projector (1 hour), Blacker Bombard (1 hour) at weekend camps in May and June 1942. He also fired a Lewis gun (13 rounds) in December 1941, a Sten in August 1942, 20 rounds of .303 in December 1941, and was 'available Tuesdays'. He had thrown live No.36M grenades in July 1942 (marked 'good'), although in December 1942 firing .30 (presumably in the P17 rifle) he was only marked as 'moderate'. There were ten more training entries up until April 1944.

However, many entries for other individuals do not show any weapons practice having been carried out, so one must assume that not all men were keen or had time to spare for such training. Generally, and for those who trained, the marking for .30 practice often indicated a 'bad' score, for example one 17-year-old member in February 1944 achieved 0 out of 13, but two months later achieved a score of 8 out of 13. One man in his twenties, who joined in April 1942, went on the 'Blitz' course at Patshull where he fired the Sten in July 1942. He also fired five rounds of .30 at 200 yards range in January 1943 and was marked 'very bad'. The EY rifle with dummy grenade was fired in February 1943, live grenades were thrown in August 1943, the Lewis gun was fired in 1943 and he attended the 'Number One Battle' (training school?) in August 1943. 'Bad' scores of 1 out of 13, 4 out of 13 and 2 out of 13 were recorded between 1943 and 1944. An attempt at firing a group of 5 rounds of .30 ammunition was described in April 1944 as a 'wash out'. Further grenade throwing led to judgments of 'moderate', 'fair/ very fair' and 'fair/ fair'. (Despite its emphasis on training, the Shrewsbury 1st Battalion could only claim that, by July 1944, 60% of its men were fully trained, the remainder being only 'semi-trained'.)

Bryan Powell remembers his father going to the Blockley's Bricks clay hole near Oakengates for firing practice. A number of plates were put up as targets for their Browning machine gun. The results were not very impressive and the Captain from the KSLI barracks at Copthorne said that he could have done more damage with his Lee Enfield rifle than the Home Guard could with their Browning![24]

Glyn Rowlands recorded that he had practical training with the Lewis gun, Sten, Tommy gun, .30 rifle, grenades and the Blacker Bombard. Part of this experience was on the range at RAF Bridgnorth. In his platoon's arsenal was a Blacker Bombard which was to be mounted on a pedestal at the junction of Berwick Road and the lane to the West Midlands Showground, covering the approach from Baschurch into Shrewsbury. He stated that they were only issued with three rounds and to move the heavy weapon from the Company's HQ it was suggested that he use his father's tradesmans' bicycle! He recollected that practical training was always a popular activity with trips to the Red Hill grenade range, Coleham drill hall .22 rifle range, the Shelton Rough and Wrekin ranges. Field training was done at Church Stretton where they roughed it in a large house on the Cardington road. Their instructors were regulars from the KSLI barracks at Copthorne. He remembers a 'dodgy' exercise at Ashes Hollow where the regulars were firing live rounds over their heads. They were carrying Stens, and at one stage they fired at full size cardboard cutouts. The Sten submachine gun was a troublesome weapon: to fire it you had to hold the magazine and not your let fingers stray to the vicinity of the ejector or cocking slot. A colleague had not heeded warnings and lost the end of a finger. The training was followed by socialising at the Woodman or Royal Oak pub at Coton. Some of his platoon eventually went into the Regular Army: Freddie Sayce was killed in Normandy, another called Holborn was commissioned and decorated as was Jock Mclaren. Ted Amos went into the RASC, Richard Smith of Butcher Row served with the Ox and Bucks Light Infantry. Rowland's turn came in 1944 when he was ordered to Canterbury to serve in the Buffs (the Royal East Kent Regiment).[25]

In Graves' *The Home Guard of Britain* there is a near-contemporary account of exercises held in the 11th Battalion area (Wellington). Various realistic exercises were held for meeting an attack of an unknown strength and from an unknown direction, points seldom brought out in local exercises. These were held with regular soldiers where the battalion put up 'a good show', the Home Guard capturing a larger Army force along with a Bren gun carrier and the Army's Commanding Officer, which gave cause for much cheering. At other exercises there was the need to explain that it was only an exercise and not an attempt to 'fell the enemy'. On one occasion a prominent piece of ground was captured, lost, then recaptured when a young Home Guard officer found that he was the only one of his rank 'surviving'. He was congratulated on his performance. 'On one occasion a company saw one of our aircraft in difficulties, the pilot had bailed out but his parachute had caught fire and he had died by the time that the Home Guard had reached him. His burning aircraft was guarded by the Home Guard for security reasons, after they had taken what they could from the plane until the arrival of Regular forces. Apparently the Home Guard had had to guard it for five hours whilst the RAF and Army argued about whose job it was to guard it!'[26]

Exercises continued to be carried out into 1944. Such a one was held in February 1944, a TEWT (tactical exercise without troops), where the whole of the 2nd Battalion was to represent German parachutists in the Stoke on Tern and Hawkstone Park area, holding the Hodnet and Wixhill road. Weapons training for the battalion carried on with, for example, the officers and men on the Llansilin range in July 1944 in competition with the .30 rifle and Browning automatic rifles, the magazines being provided on the range, as were inert No.36M grenades. Each company was to bring a Sten gun less magazine. The event proved an 'unqualified success' so a further competition was arranged for September.[27]

By the time that the war, as far as the Home Guard was concerned, was nearing its end there was a large choice of courses on offer. The No.3 GHQ Home Guard School at Onibury, commanded by Lt Col McMichael, provided three general types of courses: a general training course for company and platoon commanders; a leadership course for NCOs and junior officers; and a general training course for adjutants. Tactics and Leadership was taught at the Command School, Highdown Farm Camp, Bishops Tachbrook, Warwickshire, whilst Weapons Training was given at the Western Command Weapon Training School, Altcar, Lancashire. (Army Council Instruction No.963 mentions that officers were to bring a camp bed and bedding. PSIs, who were to be lodged in huts, were to bring blankets and 'batmen may come as long as officers do not bring their own servants'!) Another weapon training school was at Umberslade Park, Hockley Heath, Birmingham which gave instruction in 'all weapons in use by the Home Guard'. The Zone Weapon Training School, Burnhill Green, Wolverhampton, under its Commandant Major, the Earl of Dartmouth, taught range practice, tactical handling of the Spigot Mortar, use of machine guns, 'bombing', camouflage, and booby traps. Tactics was taught at the Zone Minor Tactical School, Aldridge Lodge, near Walsall, and urban warfare at the Birmingham War Office Town Training School, No.3 GHQ Town Fighting School, 130 Bristol Street, Birmingham. There was also a Battalion Commanders Course at Doddington Hall, near Nantwich; an Ammunition Officers Course No.54 at the Central Ammunition Depot School, Hewell Grange, Redditch; an Armourers Course at the Western Command Military College of Science,

Stoke; an Intelligence course at Bishops Tachbrook, Warwickshire; even a Cookery course at the Warwick Infantry Training Corps Depot. Dealing with gas poisoning was taught at the Army Gas School, Glenridding Wing, Ullswater and the Army Gas School, Winterbourne Gunner, Salisbury; Umpiring (of military exercises) at the Doddington and Onibury schools; Camouflage at Blacon Camp, Chester; whilst Interrogators had a 'time-to-time' weekend course at Birmingham University. In addition, the No.1 GHQ Home Guard School at Denbies in Surrey offered 'various courses'.[28]

Chapter 6

Morale and Discipline
in the Shropshire Home Guard

It was a regular comment during the war that 'The Home Guard is always grumbling': such a state of affairs might be expected of a force where, up to the introduction of conscription in 1942, individuals could freely leave this citizens' army. And the question of discipline in such a force, largely made up of working men, presented many problems. The possibility of Communists such as Tom Wintringham subverting this armed 'people's army' must have made many in Whitehall worry. On the other hand it has been said that changes in role required of the force (from anti-parachutist to anti-tank for example) were driven by pressures from below rather than from the upper echelons of the organisation. Throughout, there were complaints from members of the force that it was too bureaucratic and generated too much paperwork.[1]

With the onset of conscription and increasing duties there were resignations. One officer stated that he was working from 7am to 7pm on Home Guard duties. This was proving too much and he tendered a request to join the ranks. Other men resigned in anticipation of conscription. In April 1942, for example, Major Jebb wrote to a Mr Bowen at the Drill Hall, Ellesmere noting that most of Bowen's men (including Bowen himself) had resigned in anticipation of the new regulations and compulsory training, these being mostly elderly men. He pointed out that resignation from the Home Guard was now forbidden except with special permission, whilst adding that he was being discharged being aged over 65 (he was actually 67) and was to be succeeded by Major Tower.[2]

Half way through the life of the force, in April 1942, one officer in A Company (Ellesmere) of the 2nd Battalion was having second thoughts about the rural platoons. He reflected on the decline in manpower in some of the platoons, the lack of suitable leaders and the lack of time for training the men. His view that two of his Sections were felt to be 'too divergent socially to co-operate readily', sounds very strange to us in the 21st century. He went on to say: 'The above experiences have confirmed me in my original opinion, at the start of the LDV two years ago, that the organisation was not suitable for the rural platoon members of this company: there was a lack of platoon commander material. ... [Commanders must] give considerable time to the organisation, have a natural aptitude for the work, a training capacity, possess a car and a telephone and be of good social standing: if not, he is badly handicapped. Section leaders, on the other hand were more easily found. The original Home Guard [acted as] localised guerrillas, primarily to deal with parachutists at the moment of landing ... local conditions preclude the use of the rural Home Guard in any more regular capacity, for example as second-line troops to hold fixed defences off their own ground.' He expressed the view that 'training should be in guerrilla warfare and nothing else'.[3]

The relationship between officers and their men was clearly important. Major Jones, commander of D Company, found his CO, Colonel Morris Eyton, 'approachable and efficient'. Morris Eyton regarded his own role as being, somewhat enigmatically, 'the cheese in the sandwich'.[4]

The problem of the welfare of the older members in the Home Guard was addressed by its Directorate, based at the Hotel Victoria, Northumberland Avenue in London. Older men, the Directorate said, could be employed in 'clerical, stores, cooking, telephone duties and manning static weapons, for example emplaced Spigot Mortars.' However, the duty of stretcher bearing was felt not to be suitable for such men. (In terms of first aid the Home Guard, apart from having its own medical orderlies, relied on the civil medical system and had local GPs attached as Home Guard medical officers, whilst making use of local hospitals and Civil Defence first aid posts).

With the force being given, gradually, the responsibility for defending the country with the departure of more and more Regular Army troops overseas, there came an improved status. For example, in June 1943, the Commandant of the Central Ammunition Depot at Nesscliffe invited members of the 2nd Battalion to visit the Garrison Theatre there. The entertainments on offer included ENSA stage performances on Mondays and Tuesdays – ENSA standing for Entertainments National Service Association, sometimes unkindly referred to as 'Every Night Something Awful' – whilst on Thursdays and Fridays there were film shows. However entry was not free: the admission price was 3/6d (17½p), or 1 shilling (5p) if a uniform was worn. Members of the force could also be honorary members of the Sergeants' or Officers' messes.[5] The following year, in May, there was an invitation to use the canteens of the Garrison or Regular Army Institutes, but members of the Home Guard could not purchase chocolate or cigarettes 'at pre-budget prices'. Likewise, they could also use NAAFIs as long as they were in uniform.[6]

With the introduction of the woollen battle dress from late 1940 and, somewhat later, Army-style rank badges, together with the wearing of the cap badge of the county regiment, the Home Guard began to take on the appearance of its Regular brother. There was increased liaison between the Home Guard and its parent, the county regiment, plus any other military units close to particular HG battalions. As a mark of proficiency for the trained Home Guard, and after much debate, a small red felt diamond-shaped badge was introduced in April 1941, to be worn on the right sleeve. But it was to be another three years before a grudging War Office agreed to the issue of further proficiency badges: for skill at arms and for signallers. By the time that they were issued the Home Guard would only remain in existence for a further few months.[7] On the other hand, military titles could go to the

Ironbridge power station, photographed shortly after the war and before the new station was built, still showing signs of its wartime camouflage paint scheme. The Home Guard provided anti-aircraft defence, Lewis guns being positioned on each corner of the roof

heads of some and the Home Guard executive had to write and remind its members against the irregular use of military status: 'Instances have come to light of employees commissioned in the Home Guard signing documents etc of their employer with their Home Guard military status. On no occasion will signatures with a military status be used except for military matters'.[8]

Members of the force were not eligible for military decorations but could receive civil awards for bravery, for example whilst assisting in Civil Defence duties. No members of the Shropshire Home Guard was injured or killed whilst on such duties, but a significant number of members elsewhere were killed or seriously injured during the Blitz. The introduction of the Home Guard into anti-aircraft and coastal defence batteries in the middle of the war led to further casualties. (Shropshire had one anti-aircraft Home Guard unit for the defence of the Ironbridge power station, being were armed with Lewis guns mounted on the power station's roof. Its members belonged to the 6th Battalion.)

Civil medals awarded to the Home Guard countrywide were the George Medal, the British Empire Medal or the award of the MBE or OBE. Known examples of such awards in south Shropshire are those of the OBE to Lt Col Wilson, the BEM to CGMS Jones of the 3rd Battalion and Sgt Salt of the 8th Battalion. MBEs were awarded to Majors Rawson and Kayler. For less dramatic examples of exemplary service Home Guard members could be mentioned in Command Orders, or issued with Certificates of Merit, Gallantry or Good Service. For example, Certificates of Gallantry were awarded to three members of the Home Guard in south Shropshire who attempted to rescue a pilot from a crashed and burning aircraft. Other similar awards went to Major Rimmer who pushed a man out of the way of a dropped live grenade during practice in November 1943, and to Major Lovekin for a similar occurrence in December 1943. Seven Certificates for Good Service were issued to members of the 7th Battalion.[9]

The next of kin of those who died during active service could recover funeral expenses. Other, limited, benefits for the living were available, such as a temporary disablement allowance. For more serious injuries leading to discharge from the Home Guard, benefits were available under the War Pensions Warrant.[10]

On the standing down of the force in late 1944 its members received no gratuity but they were allowed to keep their warm woollen uniform which, at a time of clothing scarcity, was useful especially for those who had outdoor occupations. Members also received a certificate bearing a facsimile of George VI's signature, recording and thanking them for their period of service: Female Auxiliaries also received a certificate thanking them for their loyal service during a 'time of grievous danger', but in their case it bore the signature of the Secretary of State for War. Should they feel inclined to, members were also eligible to receive the Defence Medal but they had to make written application to receive the award.

Discipline
Not every Home Guard member was keen on his duties, although allowance needs to be made for the work pressures with which many had to cope. For those working on the land or in industry, after taking into account Home Guard parades and exercises, little time was left in the week for anything approximating to leisure. In 1940 one south Shropshire Home Guard Platoon had parades every Monday and Wednesday in the local Women's Institute hut at '7.15 pm prompt'. It was noted that some were attending regularly, whilst the attendance of others was 'not so good'.[11]

Members of the LDV/Home Guard were subject to military law under the provisions of the Army Act and liable, therefore, to prosecution for failing to fulfil their duties, but were dealt with in a civil rather than a military court. Any serious acts committed in contravention of military law whilst on active duty, however, would have been dealt with by a Court Martial. In respect of more minor infringements, except when the force would have mustered in response to an invasion and when the full provisions of the Army Act applied, any Home Guard member who was absent from duty or parade without a reasonable excuse was liable, on summary conviction in a civil court, to a fine not exceeding £10 or a maximum of one month's imprisonment or a combination of both penalties for more serious infringements.[12]

The biggest problem was absenteeism from parades and training sessions. Following the introduction of conscription a more formal disciplinary procedure had to be introduced. Witnesses would be required: merely entering the date, nature of the offence and other brief details in a register was not enough. For example, it had to be written down that the offender had been given a direct oral order or that a witness had posted a letter to the offender ordering him to attend, say, the next parade and stating the date, time and place of that parade. In the event of a continued intransigence the General Officer Commanding had to forward the necessary statements to the police so that criminal charges could be brought by them. A battalion officer was required to attend court and give evidence if necessary.[13]

The laying down of such procedures was not an idle threat, as witnessed by the prosecution of two privates in C Company the 8th Batallion at Bridgnorth on 20 June 1942. They had both failed to attend parades on 9 May and 11 May respectively. Each was fined £1.[14] On 10 August 1944, further north, another private was prosecuted. He also had been absent from parades, but presumably more frequently as a £5 fine was imposed at Oswestry Petty Sessions.[15]

As for officers who were felt not to be up to the job, a Western Command Instruction of March 1942 stated that 'unsuitable' officers were to be given three months' notice and dismissed, but only if there was good reason under Paragraph 2 of Army Council Instruction 942/40.[16]

Failure by some not to pull their weight was felt strongly by others and would have had a detrimental effect on morale. In the part of the papers of the 2nd Battalion (Oswestry), lodged in the Shropshire Archives, is an unsigned and undated letter from a Home Guardsman in Kinnerley which no doubt expressed the frustration of many others: 'What is being done about non-attenders? One man from Edgerley, Kinnerley, has only been on parade six times during the whole of his training. He didn't turn out on the 30 or 31 May. He was behind his hedge laughing at us. I say this as an old soldier. I am not the only one complaining.'[17]

In the years when our Country

was in mortal danger

LOCKLEY PERCY EVANS

who served 14th September 1943 - 31st December 1944

gave generously of his time and

powers to make himself ready

for her defence by force of arms

and with his life if need be.

George R.I.

THE HOME GUARD

The Certificate of Service issued to Lockley Percy Evans after his service in the Home Guard

Chapter 7

Mustering the Shropshire Home Guard

The fact that the majority of the Home Guard was working would have posed a problem if the force had to be mustered (it never was) as this action could disrupt disastrously industry and services, especially the railway system that served industry and contributed much to the means of defending the country. So a system of categories was introduced in 1941. In the first category were those men that could be released for an indefinite period during the duration of the emergency. In the second category were those men, especially on the railways, who were to be retained for railway operations and released only when the circumstances were such that those operations no longer needed them. In March 1942 further instructions were issued regarding mustering in an attempt to alleviate the possible ill effects on production: 'No action is to take place until hostile action has occurred, or believed to be of such evidence as to warrant the disturbance of normal conditions'. After mustering the men might be stood down so that 'daylight vocations can be carried out.'[1]

On mustering the volunteer had to bring, in addition to food (see below) his greatcoat and all equipment 'to the place where you have been instructed to report'. Other kit included a 'drinking mug and plate, with knife fork and spoon and water'. Also a 'razor, lather brush, hand brush and comb, towel, soap and toilet paper'. A change of underclothing, spare socks and hand-kerchief should be contained in a 'sand-bag'. The blanket was to be rolled 'bandolier fashion'. Ration books and identity card were to be carried. The Home Guard form 'What you MUST do when the Home Guard is mustered' allowed compensation during mustering for loss of earnings of 7 shillings (35p) per day (less for those under 18). Details of next of kin had to be provided as a precaution.

On mustering the problem of food had to be dealt with. As the Home Guard was going to fight on its own ground and retreat was not anticipated – it would either repulse the enemy or perish – the question of rations tended to focus on the short term. The scheme for feeding on mustering was outlined in June 1941 as follows: Firstly, a haversack ration for 24 hours was to be brought by each man. After 24 hours, the War Office was to issue 48 hours supply of food, consisting of 10oz of canned meat roll, 12oz of hard biscuit, an 8oz block of chocolate, 1oz of tea and 1½oz of sugar. These would be stored at each battalion HQ. Thereafter, Home Guard canteens would be established in requisitioned establishments, such as local restaurants or public houses. There was training for Home Guard cooks and catering staff but, essentially, 72 hours after mustering the organisation was largely to rely on civilian food sources.[2]

In Bishops Castle, for example, the assembly room at the Three Tuns public house was to be used as a feeding centre. Permits for the purchase of rationed food were issued to two local grocers, one dairyman and one butcher to ensure they kept sufficient food in reserve in case of mustering. The local baker was expected to supply bread for 70 men on muster. Rations for 48 hours were in hand with, of course, the provision that for the first 24 hours the Home Guard member was to rely on his own food.[3]

There was also an issue of rum to the Home Guard (or a non-alcoholic equivalent, for example tea or cocoa for teetotal members) amounting to 1/64th gallon per man. This store was, unsurprisingly, not to be held by the Home Guard units themselves but would, presumably, be issued in an emergency or during the winter months![4]

Appendix I

A Brief History of a Home Guard Company

The chronology is adapted from: 'The Official History No.5 Company 2 Battalion No 6 Zone Home Guard Queens Head Hotel, West Felton' by Major Jones dated 10 November 1944. The document is in the Shropshire Archives collection reference SA3974/173.

1940

16 July – 'invasion expected in the next few days'.

26 July – No.5 Company under the orders of the Commanding Officer the 21st Heavy Anti Aircraft Battery, Park Hall, Oswestry.

3 August – Company affiliated to KSLI.

28 August – 100 'Springfield' (P17) rifles issued in exchange for .303 rifles.

1 September – 5 rounds per man issued whilst on guard duty.

4 September – boots issued.

22 September – issue of sandbags and 'patrol bags'.

29 October – issue of serge battle dress and greatcoats.

13 November – First Lewis gun received.

1941

19 January – Sunday course at Claverley Home Guard School.

8 February – course started by the 236th Searchlight Regiment Royal Artillery, Park Hall.

11 February – red letter day: the company is allowed to fire 5 rounds from rifles and the Lewis gun.

20 April – No.5 Company respirators tested at military gas chamber, Park Hall.

6 May – tactical exercise: attack on the Maesbury defence post.

May 1941 No.5 Company platoon dispositions:

1 Platoon.   All round defence of Queens Head Bridge
2 Platoon.   In reserve at West Felton
3 Platoon.   All round defence of canal bridge, Maesbury Marsh
4 Platoon.   All round defence of Halston Bridge and block

9 June – Instruction at Claverley Home Guard School.

1942

1 March – 'No.5 Company' changed to 'D Company'.

10 May – All Dannert wire, knife rests, wire ropes collected from original strong points and brought in to reinforce the Company defence position at Queens Head Bridge.

1943

24 April – issue of Sten guns.

17 May – women auxiliaries attached to the company: 3 telephonists and 11 cooks.

10 June – Ringing of church bells as a local alarm cancelled.

28 November – Tactical exercise 'Rednal' in which RAF pilots on foot tried to reach the airfield through Home Guard cordons.

29 December – D Company dinner at West Felton Public Hall, 130 members of the Home Guard attend plus 20 guests. Menu: roast goose, salad, apple sauce, pickles, rolls and cheese, together with beer, stout, lemonade and cigarettes.

1944

12 August – 5 Vickers .30 machine guns issued.

11 September – all operational tasks and courses cease.

14 September – all roadblocks and obstacles on the highway to be dismantled or demolished.

1 November – stand down.

3 December – final parade.

Appendix II

The Organisation of the Home Guard in Shropshire

The general administration of the Shropshire Home Guard was carried out by the Territorial Army Association's Shropshire Zone HQ. All battalions were also attached to the local regiment, the King's Shropshire Light Infantry, which provided instructors and training. In addition the battalions were attached to Western Command's Welsh Border Sub District which provided information and guidance on operational matters such as the layout of defences. The sub district was itself split into a number of sub areas, each administering one or more battalions, viz:

Shrewsbury Sub Area administered the 1st and 3rd Battalions.

Oswestry Sub Area administered the 2nd Battalion.

Wellington Sub Area administered the 5th, 6th, 10th, and 11th Battalions.

South Shropshire Sub Area administered the 4th, 7th and 8th Battalions.

The Shropshire Home Guard Zone, like all other Home Guard Zones administered by the Territorial Army Association, was constantly evolving and changing. The following list therefore is merely a snapshot of the organisation as shown in a document dated September 1941 entitled 'Shropshire Zone Home Guard Location Lists'.[1]

Zone HQ: 1 Claremont Buildings, Shrewsbury
Commanding Officer: Colonel Turnbull

1st Battalion Salop Home Guard
Commanding Officer: Lt Col Dann
Battalion HQ: Morris House, Wyle Cop
Battalion Battle HQ (BHQ): Shire Hall Shrewsbury
Company Battle Headquarters:

'A' not listed
'B' Brook House, Meole Brace
'C' 1 Monkmoor Road
'D' West Midlands Electricity, Comet Bridge
'E' 40 Wood Street, Shrewsbury
'K' Junior Training Corps, Shrewsbury School
'Z' GWR Railway Station*

3rd Battalion Salop Home Guard
Commanding Officer: Lt Col Lees
Administrative Office: The Corbett Estate Market Drayton
Battalion Battle HQ: The Old Hall, Cheswardine
Company areas and location of BHQ where known:
'A' Woore
'B' Hinstock. Hinstock Manor
'C' Market Drayton. The Towers
'D' Shawbury. Foulkes Garage
'E' Hodnet
'F' Wem. The Drill Hall
'G' Prees. Prees Hall
'H' Whitchurch
'J' Ightfield

Oswestry Group Salop Home Guard

2nd Battalion Salop Home Guard
Commanding Officer: Lt Col Morris Eyton
Battalion HQ: Walford Manor, Baschurch
Battalion Battle HQ: Queens Head Hotel
Company areas and location of their Battle HQs:
'A' Ellesmere. Drill Hall, Birch Road
'B' Baschurch. Public Hall,
'C' Felton Butler. Nesscliffe Hotel
'D' West Felton. Queens Head Hotel
'E' Gobowen. Derwen Farm, St Martins
'F' Oswestry. Drill Hall
'G' Llanforda. The Vicarage, Trefonen

Officers and NCOs of D Company of the 2nd Battalion at the Queens Head Hotel, West Felton. In front of them lie two Lewis guns with skeleton butts and bipods for Home Guard use

South Shropshire Area Salop Home Guard

4th Battalion Salop Home Guard
Commanding Officer: Lt Col Gatacre
Battalion HQ: Lyth Hill
Battalion Battle HQ: The Vicarage, Bayston Hill
Company areas and BHQs where known:

        'A' Atcham. Mytton and Mermaid Hotel
        'B' Cressage. The Village Hall
        'C' Cross Houses. Fox Farm
        'D' Dorrington. The Memorial Hall, Bayston Hill
        'F' Pulverbatch. The Lion Hotel, Pontesbury
        'G' Minsterley. Mounts Nursery, Pontesbury
        'H' Wollaston. Salopian Stores, Westbury
        'J' Chirbury. The Herbert Arms
        'K' Hanwood. Lower Edgbold

7th Battalion Salop Home Guard

Commanding Officer: Lt Col Benson

Battalion Battle HQ: The Market House, Craven Arms

Company areas and location of BHQs where known:

'A' Church Stretton

'B' Craven Arms. Coton House, Clun Road

'C' Corvedale

'D' Clun

'E' Bishops Castle

'F' Ludlow. 10 Church Street

'G' Clee Hill. Tyderstone, Bitterley

'H' Burford. Ladyfield Farm, Caynham

'I' Bucknell

8th Battalion Salop Home Guard

Commanding Officer: Lt Col A.W. Foster

Battalion Battle HQ: The Drill Hall, St Mary's Street, Bridgnorth

Company areas and location of BHQs where known:

'A' Bridgnorth (East). 7 Underhill Street

'B' Bridgnorth (West)

'C' Quatt. Dudmaston

'D' Claverley. Sandford Hall

'E' Worfield. Wyken House Dairy

'F' Highley. Drill Hall

'G' Cleobury Mortimer. The Fox Inn

'H' Middleton Scriven. South Endon Farm

Wellington Group Salop Home Guard

5th Battalion Salop Home Guard

Commanding Officer: Col Oldham

Battalion HQ: The Drill Hall, King Street, Wellington

Company areas and BHQ location where known:

'A' Wellington. 20 Church Street

'B' Oakengates. Priorslee Hall, Shifnal

'C' Dawley. Town Hall

'G' 'Works'

6th Battalion Salop Home Guard
Commanding Officer: Lt Col Viscount de Vesci
Battalion HQ: The Firs, Buildwas Road, Ironbridge
Company areas and location of BHQs where known:
> 'A' Broseley
> 'B' Burwarton
> 'C' Ironbridge and Buildwas
> 'D' Madeley. Market Hall
> 'E' Much Wenlock. Talbot Garage

10th Battalion Salop Home Guard
Commanding Officer: Lt Col W.L. Foster
Battalion HQ: 4 Bradford Street, Shifnal
Company locations and BHQs where known:
> 'A' Shifnal. Drill Hall
> 'B' Albrighton
> 'C' no location given
> 'D' Kemberton. Parish Rooms
> 'E' Ryton. Beckbury Hall, Beckbury

11th Battalion Salop Home Guard
Commanding Officer: Lt Col Lovatt
Battalion Battle HQ: Harper Adams College
Company locations and BHQ locations where known:
> 'A' Newport. Newport Grammar School
> 'B' Edgmond. National Institute of Poultry
> 'C' Roden
> 'D' Great Bolas
> 'E' High Ercall

9th Battalion Salop Home Guard
This was created after September 1941 and was recruited from Post Office employees charged with protecting telephone exchanges and Post Office repeater stations in Shropshire as well as the counties of Hereford, Powys and Montgomery, and also the wireless transmitter stations at Criggion and Whitchurch, the latter also acting as a radio intercept ('Y') station. There appear to have been five Companies, 'A' to 'E'.

A number of such radio intercept stations were built during the war to intercept foreign and especially foreign wireless signals. These were, in turn, passed to Bletchley Park for decoding. That at Whitchurch was run by the Foreign and Colonial Office and intercepted Soviet broadcasts and also Japanese signals traffic in the Far East.

* This Company was part of a Great Western Railways (GWR) Battalion. In National Archives document WO199/342, it is indicated that the GWR were proposing an additional seven Battalions of Home Guard in addition to one formed in London in January 1943. One battalion was the Midland and Northern Battalion which included No.4 Company at Shrewsbury with 355 railway workers from Shrewsbury, Wellington, Craven Arms, Ludlow and Market Drayton. The HQ of No.5 Company is not given but included railway workers from Birkenhead, Saltney, Wrexham, Oswestry and Bala.[2]

Bibliography

Anon. *Shropshire War*. Shrewsbury, 2005.

Archer-Parfitt, G. (Ed). *The History of the Corps of the King's Shropshire Light Infantry (4 vols.)*. Privately published. Shrewsbury, 1968-1970.

Bilton, David. *The Home Front in the Great War*. Barnsley, 2003.

Brophy, J. *Home Guard Handbook*. London, 1943.

Brophy, J. *Britain's Home Guard: a Character Study*. London, 1945.

Carroll, D. *Dad's Army: the Home guard 1940-1944*. Stroud, 2002.

Churchill, A.W. (Capt.). *From 'Stand-to' to 'Stand-Down or with the Seventh Battalion, Shropshire Home Guard May 1940 to December 1944*. Hereford, 1946.

Collier, Basil. *The Defence of the United Kingdom*. London, 1957.

Cowan, Major J.I. *Manual of Grenades*. London, no date.

Duckers, P. *Soldiers of Shropshire*. Stroud, 2000.

Gillis, M. *Waiting for Hitler: Voices from Britain on the Brink of Invasion*. London, 2007.

Graves, C. *The Home Guard of Britain*. London, 1943.

Hunt. R. *Uniforms of the Home Guard*. Storrington, West Sussex, 2002.

Ingleton, Roy. *The Gentlemen at War: Policing Britain 1939-45*. 1994, Maidstone.

Jones, C., Lowry, B., Wilks, M. *Twentieth Century Defences in Britain: the West Midlands*. Logaston, Herefordshire, 2008.

Kieser, E. *Hitler on the Doorstep: Operation Sealion: the German Plan to Invade Britain 1940*. London, 1997.

Langdon-Davies, J. *Home Guard Warfare*. London, 1941.

Lowry, B. *British Home Defences, 1940-45*. Oxford, 2004.

Mackenzie, S.P. *The Home Guard*. Oxford, 1995.

Marshall-Cornwall, James. *Wars and Rumours of Wars*. London, 1984.

Mills, J. and Carney, C. *In the Space of a Single Day: the Insignia and Uniforms of the LDV and Home Guard 1940-1944 and 1952-1956*. London, 2001.

Stettinius, E.R. (jr). *Lend Lease*. Harmondsworth, 1944.

Street, A.G. *From Dusk Till Dawn*. London, 1943.

West, Nigel. *MI5: British Security Service Operations 1909-1945*. London, 1988.

Wheeler, Rob (ed.). *German Invasion Plans for the British Isles 1940* (edited facsimile). Oxford, 2007.

References

Chapter 1 The Local Defence Volunteers in Shropshire

1. Duckers, pp.7-8
2. Bilton
3. Ingleton, p.85
4. www.staffshomeguard.co.uk
5. Churchill, pp.10-11
6. Archer-Parfitt, p.355
7. Graves, p.316
8. SA1024/197
9. SA5483/1 and 101/1
10. SA1024/198
11. SA1024/199
12. SA1024/201
13. SA1024/203
14. SA1024/400
15. SA4861/1/1
16. SA4861/3/99
17. www.staffshomeguard.co.uk
18. Archer-Parfitt, p.355
19. SA4861/3/59
20. Stettinius, pp.35-38 and pp.59-60
21. SA1024 /105- /112
22. 'Dad's Army at Wistanstow', *Shropshire Magazine*, September 1980
23. SA1024/80-90
24. SA1024/1
25. SA1024/80-103
26. SA1024/86
27. SA1024/87
28. Wheeler, p.67
29. Marshall-Cornwall, p.197
30. NA WO166/94
31. SA2671/13
32. SA 1024/96
33. SA1024/93
34. SA486/1/1
35. SA4861/3/102
36. SA4861/3/33
37. West, pp.184-196
38. From an account in the *Shropshire Star* of 17 February 2001
39. SA5483/1 and 101/1
40. SA4861/3/68, 101/1 and 3974/173
41. SA4861/2/4
42. Graves, pp.318 and 359

Chapter 2 The Home Guard in Shropshire

1. SA4861/3/39
2. SA1024 /124
3. SA1024/105, /115, /118 and /125
4. SA4861/3/68
5. SA4861/3/34
6. SA4861/3/39
7. SA4861/3/103
8. Shropshire Regimental Museum File 70
9. Graves, p.318
10. Graves, p.316
11. SA1024/47
12. 'Dad's Army at Wistanstow' *The Shropshire Magazine* September 1980
13. SA4861/3/108
14. 'Dad's Army at Wistanstow' *The Shropshire Magazine* September 1980
15. SA4861/3/104 and SA4861/105
16. SA4861/2/32
17. SA4861/3/33
18. SA1024/137
19. SA1024 /141
20. SA1024/149
21. SA1024/149
22. SA4861/3/36
23. SA1024/148
24. SA4861/3/146
25. SA4861/3/107 and /109
26. SA1024/174
27. SA3216/13
28. SA4861/169
29. SA1024/153 and /163
30. From an account in the *Shropshire Star* of 17 February 2001
31. SA4861/3/137 and SA4861/3/135
32. SA2671/29
33. SA4861/3/65
34. SA1474 Box III. Fuller details of the stop lines, anti-tank islands and defended localities that existed in Shropshire in the Second World War are given in *Twentieth Century Defences in Britain: the West Midlands* by Colin Jones, Bernard Lowry and Mick Wilks
35. SA4861/3/65

36. Shropshire Regimental Museum File 70
37. SA1024/66
38. Churchill, pp.26-27 and 29
39. Shropshire Regimental Museum File 70
40. SA4861/3/114
41. Graves, p.139 and Army Council Instruction 872 of April 1942
42. SA4861/3/65
43. SA1024/224
44. SA1474/59
45. Home Guard Instruction 48 of 1942
46. SA1355/13 and SA14861/3/147
47. SA4861/3/48 and SA4861/3/66
48. SA4861/3/67
49. SA4861/3/68
50. SA1474/159
51. Archer-Parfitt, p.358
52. Churchill, p.37 and SA3974/173
53. Graves, pp.359-360
54. SA4861/3/174
55. Anon., *Shropshire's War* and also information from the Commonwealth War Graves Commission: 'Casualties of the Home Guard Who Died Whilst on Official Duty.'
56. Archer-Parfitt, p.359

Chapter 3 Arming the Shropshire Home Guard

1. K.R. Gulvin, *The Kent Home Guard*, (Rainham, 1980)
2. SA2671/6 HGI no 50
3. SA974/173
4. SA4861/3/59
5. Shropshire Regimental Museum File 70
6. HGI 48
7. SA4861/3/112
8. Conversation with John Hughes, 28 February 2002
9. Mackenzie, p.97
10. SA1024/217 and 1024/244
11. SA4861/3/116
12. SA1024/193
13. SA1024/84
14. SA1024/85
15. SA1474/1
16. SA1474 box 1/184
17. SA101/1
18. SA4861/3/33

19. SA4861/3/ 119-122
20. SA2376/2/7-12
21. Undated plan in author's collection
22. SA1474 box 1 /112
23. SA1024/47
24. SA1024/222
25. SA4861/3/97
26. SA101/1

Chapter 4 Equipment and Communications for the Shropshire Home Guard

1. SA4861/3/59
2. Mills and Carney, p.51
3. SA1024/196 and Churchill, p.22
4. Shropshire Regimental Museum File 70
5. Graves, p.317
6. SA4861/2/1-3
7. SA1024/42
8. SA1024/173
9. SA1024/47
10. SA4861/3/55
11. SA1024/40
12. SA4861/3/148
13. Anon., *Shropshire's War*
14. SA4861/3/88
15. SA1024/65, 1024/73 and 1474/83
16. SA4861/3/138
17. SA1474/83, 4861/3/65 and 101/1
18. SA4861/3/142 and 4861/3/41-43

Chapter 5 Training the Shropshire Home Guard

1. SA1024/197
2. Graves, p.318
3. SA 3216/13
4. Graves, pp.314-5
5. SA1474/59
6. SA1024/47
7. SA2933/7
8. SA4861/16
9. SA1474/59
10. SA4861/2/18
11. Conversation with Bryan Powell, 5 June 2008
12. Conversation with Lockley Percy Evans, 6 May 2002
13. SA4861/2/19
14. SA1024/ 1829

15. Shropshire Regimental Museum File 70
16. SA4861/36
17. SA4861/37
18. SA4861/3/43
19. SA4861/2/22-28
20. Shropshire Regimental Museum File 70
21. SA4861/2 /29
22. SA4861/2/31
23. Home Guard Instruction 48 of 1942
24. Conversation with Bryan Powell, 5 June 2008
25. Personal communication, 30 March 1996
26. Graves, p.317
27. SA861/3/68
28. SA2671/3 and 1474/60

Chapter 6 Morale and Discipline in the Shropshire Home Guard
1. Brophy (1945), pp.35-36
2. SA4861/3/28
3. SA4861/3/23 and 4861/3/22
4. SA4861/3/124 and 3974/173
5. SA4861/3/24
6. SA4861/3/50 and 1024/40
7. Mills and Carney, pp.36-38

8. SA4861/3/47
9. Churchill, pp.72-74
10. Army Council Instruction (ACI) 872 of 1942
11. SA1024/206
12. ACI 924 of 1940, amended ACI 872 of 1942
13. SA4861/3 /91
14. SA1474/63
15. SA4861/3/68
16. SA1474/ 45
17. SA4861/3/90

Chapter 7 Mustering the Shropshire Home Guard
1. SA4861/3/71 and 1474 Box 1
2. SA4861/3/110
3. SA1024/52 and 1024/69
4. SA1024/218

Appendix II The Organisation of the Home Guard in Shropshire
1. SA4861/3/30
2. I am grateful to Mick Wilks for this information

Index